DON'T SAY SORRY

DON'T SAY SORRY

MAKE GREAT DECISIONS, WITHOUT REGRETS

TIM BAKKEN

Post Hill PRESS

A POST HILL PRESS BOOK
ISBN: 979-8-89565-482-8
ISBN (eBook): 979-8-89565-483-5

Don't Say Sorry:
Make Great Decisions, Without Regrets

Cover design by Jim Villaflores

Post Hill Press
New York • Nashville
posthillpress.com

Published in the United States of America
1 2 3 4 5 6 7 8 9 10

TABLE OF CONTENTS

INTRODUCTION

THE DECISION-MAKING FORMULA

(SEARCHING FOR CORRECT ANSWERS)

Once, after seeing a childhood friend in a difficult position, I understood well how our lives would be very different if at just one of the critical moments we had made a better decision. One job instead of another would have produced more or less satisfaction, the way a different partner or spouse would have led to a shorter or longer marriage and produced children with different abilities and personalities. I thought that perhaps through experiences or ancient documents I could find something that dictated how to make smart decisions, or, better yet, correct decisions. Just as disheartening as the absence of wisdom about good decision-making was my observation that everyone is constantly at risk of being harmed by seven fundamentals of failure that can doom personal and professional relationships.

It is ironic then that an incident more than forty years ago, in a maximum-security prison of all places, provided the theme for this book, that correct decision-making will lead to an enriching life. While in law school, I worked in a legal assistance program helping prison inmates in their parole hearings. One day, about a dozen fellow students and I, along with a supervisor, were guided by an assistant warden and toured what seemed like a prehistoric prison that should have had dinosaurs flying around it. Opened in 1854, it remains operational today, housing eight hundred inmates in Waupun, Wisconsin.

We met with staff members and visited the food service area, the gym, cell blocks, and administrative segregation, sometimes known as the hole, where the most recalcitrant prisoners are confined in isolation, seeing only a few prison staff members and no one else, a condition that, as you will see, leads to early death for anyone who experiences it. We walked among prisoners who, in jumpsuits, were required to walk more than an arm's length away from non-prisoners, a distance like long bird wings flapping. The assistant warden stopped us in front of an open, unoccupied cell with bars and pointed to its features: bunk beds, a toilet and a sink the size of a small bowl, a chair, and a ledge protruding from a wall, everything metal.

We formed a half-circle around the assistant warden, who stood at the entrance of the cell and faced us. I stood behind the other students, with our backs to the prisoners, who were walking along the wide corridor behind us. I had played on high school and college basketball teams, and looking sideways had become routine. Glancing side-eye left, I noticed a scraggily-haired inmate in his baggy clothes using a wet mop to clean the floor behind us. He moved from left to right. I lost sight of him for a moment and then saw him again, side-eye right.

He started mopping back toward us, swishing over territory he had covered. He was directly to my right side, and if I had flapped my arm, I would have touched him. The assistant warden talked more slowly as he watched the prisoner, and the other students in the front swiveled their heads to see what the warden saw. I turned right and looked directly at the young man, who stopped mopping.

My brain instructed me to speak, but he beat me to it.

"Bakken," my last name, he growled.

"Johnny," I said.

Reflexively, I asked him, "How's it going?"

"How does it look like it's going?"

I smiled and was glad to see him, though I sensed the assistant warden did not want any more dialogue between us. "It is great to see you," I said.

"Same."

He mopped the same concrete again as he drifted away. Before he turned his back, he smiled.

Misfortune, I learned, can find all of us. Eight years earlier, I had been new to a high school in my junior year, in a small city bisected by a river, surrounded by country. I had an old car, and, after basketball practices, Johnny (pseudonym) would wait for me and ask for a ride home, about ten miles out on rural roads, often with only a few other cars. The guys who had known him for years would tell me not to talk to or give him a ride anywhere because he was a troublemaker. He was all of that, and he went on to do many bad things.

At the end of the main, paved country road where he lived, you could see the silhouette of his three-story house, down a hill via a dirt road. I didn't like driving down that dirt road, icy and slippery in the winter and muddy during the thaw. The sky was dark when we arrived. No lights were on. I did not see a parent or other person or any barn or farm animals, not baying dogs or feral cats. Empty fields surrounded the house on three sides. The car would bounce a few times over moguls before I'd stop it short of snow drifts, boards with rusty nails, sawhorses, or downed tree branches. Though we'd talk about teachers and classmates, Johnny would leave the car and shut the door without saying goodbye, not smiling, not looking back as he shuffled toward the house.

I have not seen or spoken to him since that day in the prison, and I couldn't find any court records to indicate why he was incarcerated then. But more recent records show that he received a fifteen-year prison sentence for a serious crime and remains in prison today. I did find two court records from 1974 that reported on a man who died in 1974 and had the same first name, last name, and middle initial as Johnny. The records indicate that the man's estate, and that doesn't necessarily mean big, nice, or expensive, only that he had property, was processed through a probate court when Johnny would have been seventeen years old. That was about when I gave him rides home to the dark house. It appears that Johnny might have inherited his father's homestead and lived there alone, with no family, during high school, when our paths crossed, prior to our one meeting in the prison.

Johnny and I probably started at about the same place in life, though he encountered problems that made his pathway more treacherous. I had heard but couldn't confirm that back then he had been imprisoned for stealing cars. Without knowing of his isolation at the house in the country, an outsider could not understand how Johnny's desperation as a teenager could produce a car thief and then later someone who would go on to commit other crimes, including the most serious one when he was fifty-seven years old.

Though bad decisions leading to imprisonment might seem distant, you will be required to make life-or-death decisions. For instance, an elderly person who enters a nursing home, a kind of confinement, will die sooner than if she had remained in her own home, and, on average, sooner than one year after entering the facility, as you will see. How can you know what to decide for your mother, father, or partner, perhaps for yourself? Though you can find elsewhere plausible methods on how to make decisions, in this book you will find four pillars of decision-making that can lead to an enriching and happy life if you believe they are right for you and act according to your conscience: (1) recognition of your top ability; (2) implementation of a problem-solving method, such as the Decision-Making Formula; (3) avoidance of the seven fundamentals of failure; and (4) knowledge of the elements of happiness.

The lessons from the life-or-death stories ahead are universal and will help you resolve inevitable challenges and make correct decisions when you confront emergencies. In this book, the strongest recommendation is that, in finding what's right for you, begin by acknowledging one unwavering fact: Your success and enrichment, especially happiness or whatever you call your most meaningful state of mind, can be complete only through having close relationships with other people.

You'll see over and over through the studies and stories ahead that close relationships—and they needn't be defined like marriage or be predictable unions of groups, clubs, or teams—are the roots of everything good. You might need different relationships at different times. Regrettably, the teenage friendship between Johnny and me was not sufficient to steer him in the right direction. Though able to survive, but not yet a man, Johnny obviously needed much more than a car ride to an empty house to avoid the grip of isolation, as much as an octogenarian needs much more after seeing most of her close friends pass away before her eyes. If you take away one thing from this book, it is this: try to develop relationships in which you can be confident that the people close to you will be there when you need them, including at the end.

My work over the decades has put me in contact with many people who have had to make life-or-death decisions. As a homicide prosecutor, my work with police officers, medical examiners, witnesses of killings, families of deceased victims, and the killers themselves showed the grave implications of bad decision-making. Though I didn't know it at the time, I once worked with the most dangerous police officer in American history, a New York City police detective who worked a side job as a hitman for the Mafia. For the past twenty-six years, I've worked at the US Military Academy, West Point, as its longest-serving professor of law, and glimpsed the reason why the last American victory in a war occurred in 1945.

Some of the events reported in this book should contribute to your making more correct decisions or, when a problem is complicated, your selection of a few best options among many. In addition to making correct decisions, though, you will want to try to avoid the seven fundamentals of failure. To this end, chapter one introduces two inherent fundamentals of failure, human error and incompetence. In chapter two, you'll see the fundamental of falsity in other people. Chapter three tells the story of highly competent people who decide to act against their conscience, which introduces falsity into their own lives. Chapter four shows how to handle the most emotionally draining fundamentals of failure, silence and fear, as well as the demoralization that accompanies them.

Chapter five describes the consequences when a fragile person allows other people to control his decisions. Chapter six, practically and metaphorically, is devoted to finding competent people who can save you from the bacteria that would be deadly if not for the antibiotics created by smart scientists; there are relatively few of them in the world. Chapter seven describes the ten elements of happiness and the importance of avoiding isolation. Chapter eight, the conclusion, applies the Decision-Making Formula to the end-of-life decisions you will need to make for the people closest to you and for yourself.

THE DECISION-MAKING FORMULA

The importance of correct decision-making illustrates the urgency in finding a method through which to do it. Ian Watson, a mathematician, in a 2013 book, pointed to "17 Equations That Changed the World," including Pythagoras's Theorem, the Law of Gravity, and Relativity.[1] Equations like these provide somewhat definitive rules because they lead to mathematical, geometric, and physical discoveries that can be measured or observed, like black holes and atomic reactions.

In contrast, you cannot easily observe or measure the operations inside your brain—that is, whether you maximized your natural ability and reached the best decision possible. Nonetheless, though you can't see gravity, you know it exists, and, similarly, you know that some decisions are better than others. Therefore, in trying to identify a way to resolve your most important matters, like a scientist measuring how much thrust is necessary to beat gravity, you can similarly rely on the new Decision-Making Formula to find what's right for you:

> If (natural abilities + attributes of success) + (observations/practices) > (fundamentals of failure) = correct decision-making.

In essence, if you can identify and apply your best characteristics and not allow the fundamentals of failure to overwhelm them, then you will make correct decisions. That process, which should be imbued with your aspirations and dreams, is represented in the figure below.

If [Abilities] + [Attributes] + [Observations] > [Fundamentals of Failure] = [Correct Decision-Making]

Abilities	Attributes	Observations	Fundamentals of Failure
Math	Humility	Practices	Silence
Verbal	Empathy	Experiences	Human Error
Spatial/	Fairness	Trial/Error	Incompetence
Perceptual	Trust		Isolation
			Inaction
			Fear
			Falsity

If the positive variables (abilities, attributes, and observations) outweigh the negative variables (fundamentals of failure), then you may consider your decision to be correct.

As in the figure above, the three natural abilities are mathematical, verbal, and spatial (perception) (MVP).

To those abilities, you should add the attributes of your success, the ways you've learned to act—humility, empathy, fairness, and trust (build HEFT).

To the abilities and attributes, add your observations of events and your practices, essentially your trials and errors, which can also be referred to as experience.

The positive variables—your abilities, attributes, and observations/practices—can be diminished by the negative variables, the seven fundamentals of failure: silence, human error, incompetence, isolation, inaction, fear, and falsity (avoid SHIIIFF). If, on the left side of the = sign, the positive variables are greater than (>) the negative variables, then the decision, on the right side of the = sign, should indicate a correct decision.

Simply, you can use the Decision-Making Formula to resolve your issues. Over many years, though, commentators have recommended that you adopt a large number of presumably positive characteristics that they have identified: be resilient, gritty, vulnerable, team-oriented, and self-aware. Learn to know when to start or quit a business, endeavor, or relationship. However, the inapplicability of others' recommendations to your specific issues may distract you from identifying and developing the best characteristics within yourself.

In 2001, for example, Jim Collins authored the popular book *Good to Great: A Study of Management Strategies of Companies with Lasting Growth*. Collins, importantly, teaches how to simplify the goals of companies. Simplification helps to limit distractions and the number and variability of the tasks that employees, or anyone, must perform. Like a hedgehog, according to Collins, people and companies should "understand that the essence of profound insight is simplicity," and he uses Einstein's equation, $e = mc^2$, as an example.[2]

Collins is on firm ground when he concludes that top leaders embody humility and "unwavering resolve."[3] But, like many commentators, he, too, is less instructive when he uses analogies to try to help people visualize positive actions. Collins's most popular analogy, relied on by others, is the flywheel, a way to compare the operations of a mechanical device to the operations of people or a business.[4] A flywheel is a heavy, metal wheel that is attached to a rotating shaft and, through inertia, stores energy for intermittent use. Collins describes it as follows: "Picture a huge, heavy flywheel—a massive metal disk mounted horizontally on an axle, about 30 feet in diameter, 2 feet thick, and weighing about 5,000 pounds. Now imagine that your task is to get the flywheel rotating on the axle as fast and long as possible. Pushing with great effort, you get the flywheel to inch forward, moving almost imperceptibly at first.... Then, at some point—breakthrough! The momentum of the thing kicks in your favor, hurling the flywheel forward, turn after turn... whoosh!"[5]

While the flywheel analogy is visually memorable, and Collins is adept at explaining the mechanical process, the analogy is not applicable to human behavior or decision-making. A metal machine's inanimate operations are not similar to the mental processes that people use to arrive at decisions and then act. Instead of visualizing machines or trying futilely to adopt the recommended characteristics of commentators—vulnerability and extreme ownership have been popular—you will be better served by developing your own abilities and attributes and, simultaneously, avoiding the pitfalls to which other people expose you. Your selection of jobs, employees, companies, teams, friends, partners, and spouses is an individual decision that should be influenced by your nature and organized by a method or formula. In other words, after thorough preparation, can you act according to what you believe is right for you and the organizations and people to whom you've made a commitment? That is not a mechanical operation. It is a decision.

Correct decisions, though, will be less fulfilling if they are not accompanied by enrichment and happiness. In a 2020 study, researchers answered what may be the most important inquiry into human development, which they considered to be "Question #1":

> Is there an ability threshold, beyond which more ability doesn't matter? No [they answered]. While other things are certainly required for all important life accomplishments, greater ability leads to greater achievement.[6]

Someone with greater ability, all other things equal, will have greater success than someone else with less ability.

You should assess this finding carefully to avoid the demoralization that might accompany the universal fear that, in comparison to others, you are not smart or strong enough to accomplish your goals. A 1998 study, influential but misapplied, indicated that such a feeling could inhibit performance and satisfaction:

> Six studies demonstrated that praise for intelligence had more negative consequences for students' achievement motivation than praise for effort. Fifth graders praised for intelligence were found to care more about performance goals relative to learning goals than children praised for effort. After failure, they also displayed less task persistence, less task enjoyment, more low-ability attributions, and worse task performance than children praised for effort.[7]

That study's conclusion made it appear that teachers' praise for students' effort is more important than praise for students' natural intellectual development. However, the study contributed to a mistaken belief that became prevalent in American education and culture, that praise for effort should supplant praise for performance.

You needn't be defensive about your limitations, but you should recognize which ones you possess. In a commencement speech in 1974, the Nobel-Prize winning physicist Richard Feynman, regarding scientific integrity, emphasized the importance of reflection and humility. He said, "The first principle is that you must not fool yourself—and you are the easiest person to fool."

Rectify your shortcomings, if possible, but you will be better served in the long run by identifying and applying your strongest natural characteristics. Professor Adam Grant, an organizational psychologist, described what happened when society devalued performance and overvalued effort:

> The idea of lauding persistence quickly made its way into [articles, books, and talks and]...reinforced the

> American dream that with hard work, anyone could achieve success.... The problem is that we've taken the practice of celebrating industriousness too far. We've gone from commending effort to treating it as an end in itself. We've taught a generation of kids that their worth is defined primarily by their work ethic. We've failed to remind them that working hard doesn't guarantee doing a good job.[8]

In essence, people who do not accurately assess their strengths and weaknesses do not fully develop their top ability, whether it's mathematical, verbal, or perceptual.

Incorrect decisions waste time, your most valuable resource. A 2024 study measuring persistence found "that high-grit individuals persevere in pursuing unsolvable problems in tasks having no time limit but not in tasks having a time limit."[9]

If you do not recognize your strengths or assess correctly what can be accomplished, you will waste time on activities that provide relatively few or no benefits to you individually or to your businesses and families. Grit, whatever it is, is not useful without the ability to know when to stop or redirect your effort.

Professor Grant concluded, "There's a reason we award Olympic medals to the athletes who swim the fastest, not the ones who train the hardest. What counts is not sheer effort but the progress and performance that result. Motivation is one of multiple variables in the achievement formula. Ability, opportunity, and luck count, too. Yes, you can get better at anything, but you can't be great at everything."[10]

Accordingly, the researchers in the 2020 study into human development posed another critical question, whether you can improve:

> Beyond ability, interest, and opportunity, are conative attributes [desire, effort, and initiative] important?

They answered *yes.*[11] However, their explanation of how improvement occurs, while commonsensical, leads to a third question before completely answering the second question. How much are you willing to sacrifice for a relationship, career, or business, or even for your children?

The researchers, professors David Lubinski and Camilla P. Benbow, concluded, in answering the second question, that "the inordinate amount of time truly outstanding performers give to their craft" is the variable that separates them from ordinary and other high performers. "Those exceptional individuals at the forefront of their disciplines, who routinely advance creative products, and take on demanding leadership roles at premier universities, scientific and technical institutes, major law firms, and industry (to list but a few) do not just put in 40-hour work weeks."[12]

Some find solace in begrudging highly successful or wealthy people the fruits of their labor or good fortune, but the researchers, after considering ability, were more neutral and concerned primarily with the costs to society of individuals' lack of desire to improve themselves. "Just like people in general, exceptionally talented populations view opportunities and the associated tradeoffs differently. Being at the top of one's profession requires a certain lifestyle that for many involves making some hard decisions, such as less time with family or for leisure. This is one of the reasons why truly outstanding creative and occupational accomplishments are so rare."[13] Thus, once you identify your top ability and learn to optimize it, the answer to the third question, how much am I willing to sacrifice, depends on how you prioritize the activities in your life.

THE FOUR ATTRIBUTES OF CORRECT DECISION-MAKING

Along with the three abilities that researchers have found are the steel girders of material success (mathematical, verbal, and perceptual), the most successful people have learned how to enhance in themselves and develop in others four attributes:

- Humility—recognizing one's limitations and not being defensive.
- Empathy—understanding the motivations and feelings of others.
- Fairness—treating others based on their thinking and actions.
- Trust—disclosing facts to help others alleviate their worries.

We'll find that the best leaders possess all four of the attributes. That's not to say that leaders must generate warmth, but they should create an environment that welcomes curiosity and exploration by everyone around them.

Not well known outside his profession, Myron E. Ullman III, who died in 2024 from Alzheimer's disease and cancer at age seventy-seven, produced popular products because he employed the attributes in the Decision-Making Formula. During his career, Ullman had been a top executive at retail companies, Macy's, J.C. Penney, Starbucks, and LVMH, a French company with brands that include Louis Vuitton, Bulgari, Dior, Fendi, and Givenchy. Insiders marveled at his curiosity, insight, and persistence, though Ullman's wife said shopping with him could be disappointing because of those characteristics. "He was only ever interested in analyzing a store's layout, customer service and merchandise offerings," the *New York Times* reported in Ullman's obituary.[14]

Ullman and his wife, Cathy Emmons, married in 1969 and had six children. She said of her husband, "When you went to a store with him, you weren't shopping. You were just walking the store to see how everything worked."[15]

Almost no one remarked on Ullman's likeability, though there was little or no evidence he was not kind and decent. The founder of Starbucks, Howard Schultz, said of Ullman, "He never sought the spotlight, and he really defined for me and others what servant leadership truly means. The success that Starbucks enjoyed while he was the lead director, and at my side, is very hard to even measure. It's incomparable."

At Macy's, Ullman, beginning in 1988, "stocked stores with merchandise that more closely reflected the tastes…of local shoppers" and used computers to assess customers' buying patterns, two decades or more before the practice became widespread.[16]

Under Ullman's leadership, in 2005, J.C. Penney's operating profit increased 22.5 percent. After Penney's success, a takeover firm bought the company and fired Ullman, but, after losses, it hired him back.

Professor Jeffrey Sonnenfeld, from the Yale School of Management, said of Ullman, "He was very good about doing the dirty work, the operational stuff, making sure that store operations were working functionally well."[17] By all accounts, Ullman possessed HEFT—humility, empathy, fairness, and trust—and these four positive attributes were the cornerstones of his leadership.

THE SEVEN FUNDAMENTALS OF FAILURE

Myron Ullman was successful because he created conditions that allowed other people to advance according to their abilities, attributes, and experience, and you can learn to identify and associate with such people. Similarly, though at the other end of the desirability spectrum, you can identify what causes failure in an organization or a person. The reason for decline can almost always be traced to one of the seven fundamentals of failure, which are detailed in the stories in the chapters ahead.

Among the seven fundamentals, *fear* and *silence* prevent people from speaking and acting according to their conscience. *Incompetence* includes not performing to the level of your ability or not avoiding those who can hurt you. *Isolation* concerns being more alone than you wish or not having access to someone who understands you. *Inaction* is your unwillingness to risk losing something despite the possibility of significant advancement by trying something different. *Falsity* is knowingly accepting conditions (or people) that do not feel right to you.

The most common fundamental of failure is *human error*, which is present in the next story and will help you to begin to identify your top abilities and attributes. In my job at the US Military Academy, in the spring semester of 2006, cadet Sara Knutson, a junior, sat in the front row in one of my criminal law classes. Unlike most cadets who endure four grueling years of a controlling, conforming college experience, she smiled every day. Cadets are transactional, "cooperate and graduate," they say, and they get away from just about any obligation as soon as possible, good luck and goodbye, and they're gone, though not always.

The next academic year, I was on sabbatical, which is a year away from teaching to conduct research or participate in professional activities. I spent part of that time in Kabul, Afghanistan, creating the law department at a new military academy. When I returned to West Point, a thank-you card from Cadet Knutson, who was nearing her May 2007 graduation, awaited me. As with the cards and notes I've received from students from time to time over the years,

I saved this one, too, without knowing how much it would mean to me later. Knutson wrote, "Prof. Bakken, Sir, while it's been a while since I've had you as a teacher with your absence this year, your class is still one of the most memorable of all my classes at West Point. I loved criminal law. Thank you for making class interesting and for all that you've done for the cadets here. Respectfully, Sara Knutson."

That she wrote and sent the card was as meaningful as her generous words. She graduated and branched aviation, which requires an extensive training period and extra years of service in the army beyond the usual five-year stint. (The current obligation for aviation officers is twelve years.) Knutson became a Black Hawk helicopter pilot and was plunked down in the middle of the war in Afghanistan. In November 2012, she married a fellow army officer.

On March 11, 2013, Knutson, promoted to captain, twenty-seven years old, was piloting a Black Hawk on a training mission in Kandahar, Afghanistan. The war was then eleven and a half years long, when it should have been over, but it was on its way to twenty years, ending in 2021, the Taliban in firmer control of Afghanistan than when US forces invaded in 2001.

Knutson, the crew leader, was operating the helicopter in a heavy rainstorm during a training mission. No one knows exactly what happened. Somehow, the Black Hawk whirled and crashed, killing all its occupants, Captain Knutson and four other soldiers.

Her husband, himself a former Black Hawk pilot and by then a private contractor working in Afghanistan, accompanied her body back to the United States. In announcing her death, the last line in a West Point publication read: "[Captain Sara Knutson Cullen's] mother remembers her as an adventurous, fun-loving young woman with a smile and a laugh that would light up a room."

In the fall semester of 2023, another former student who had taken the criminal law course, a 2019 graduate, was back at West

Point for an event. She stopped by my office to reminisce and tell me about her army career. She, too, had sent me a card of thanks prior to graduation and, like Knutson, had sat in the front row of the class. In one of the coincidences of life, and it's not clear whether the symmetry is welcome, she told me that she had branched aviation and become the pilot of a Black Hawk helicopter.

Like Knutson, she was now an army captain, with her own helicopter and crew. She explained that, given her years in the army and the career trajectory of a pilot, there was likely only one year remaining for her to gain combat experience. After that, she would become a commander, spending most of her time training soldiers to fly helicopters. Army officers don't want to see war, but, like heart surgeons, police officers, and ambulance drivers, few of whom want harm to come to anyone, they want an opportunity to practice their craft.

In our conversation, I told the captain the story of Sara Knutson and mentioned the coincidence that both of them took the elective course in criminal law. But that was one of the stories I wish I hadn't told because maybe it put some worry in her mind. The chance that two women, though in different decades, from one course would both become Black Hawk pilots, a job dominated by men, is small. There are at least seventeen other helicopters used by the US military.[18] In 2019, only 8.3 percent of Black Hawk pilots (258 out of 3,117) were women.[19] I'll worry about that symmetry until the living Black Hawk pilot leaves the army. She and Knutson shared the same first name.

In the spring semester of 2024, I was again teaching the course, and one of the cadets who had missed classes because she played on an athletic team that traveled frequently wanted to meet to prepare for an exam. In our meeting, she asked questions and described legal principles to ensure she was on the right track of study. I was surprised because, despite missing classes, she grasped the material quickly. To end our meeting, I asked whether the insignia on her collar indicated that she would become an army doctor.

"No," she said, "That's aviation."

"Congratulations." I thought for another second before speaking. "That is a coincidence, because two other women who took this course branched aviation. What are your plans?"

"I'd like to fly a Black Hawk," she said.

"The other aviators became captains and flew Black Hawks," I told her. "You'll have a great career."

The next semester, fall 2024, a few minutes after the final exam in December, another cadet who had also missed classes because she had traveled with her teammates to athletic events, approached me with a smile as big as that of Sara Knutson's. "Sir," she said, "remember how I promised to tell you what branch I would serve in?"

"Yes. You were hoping for aviation."

She pulled the lapel on her shirt to indicate her branch's insignia, which the previous semester I had mistaken for the medical corps (doctors) because both the medical corps and aviation insignias have wings.

"I'll be an aviator, flying Black Hawks."

I offered my congratulations, telling her about the coincidence of women from the course becoming Black Hawk pilots. Including Captain Knutson, six of my former students, as lieutenants or captains, died in the wars in Afghanistan and Iraq.[20] Sometimes decisions can be tragically wrong. You'll see the reason why is that either someone was lacking an essential ability, attribute, or experience, or, despite possessing all those positive variables, that person was overwhelmed by one or more of the seven fundamentals of failure.

The Black Hawk helicopter in Afghanistan, an inanimate object, like a flywheel that operates mechanically, did not crash of its own volition. A human error might have come from someone in the helicopter, the decision of an officer on the ground to allow the crew to fly in bad weather, a faulty repair by a mechanic, or the decisions of two presidents to that point in time, Bush and Obama, to continue the war. The cause was most likely the culmination of those kinds of misjudgments, as well as others unknown.

We might not know which error was most connected to the crash. Still, you can learn from the Black Hawk pilots to prepare diligently and find a method like the Decision-Making Formula to learn how to identify and then optimize your top abilities and attributes and work your hardest on every task while avoiding the seven fundamentals of failure. I know that the Black Hawk pilots, when they graduated, possessed top abilities and attributes and would work diligently so they'd never need to tell the soldiers under their command, "I'm sorry." Whatever decisions you make, like the pilots, you'll want to know that you did your best and acted according to your conscience.

Key Points

- The Decision-Making Formula can help you make correct decisions.
- Your top ability will lead you to more success, but you need to identify it.
- Wise risk-taking produces more enrichment.
- Act according to your conscience so you don't do someone else's bidding.
- The seven fundamentals of failure must be avoided.

CHAPTER 1

LOSS LEADER—LIFE IS GOOD, BELIEVE ME

(CONFRONTING HUMAN ERROR)

In studying and applying the Decision-Making Formula, you'll find that despite the presence of the positive variables—abilities, attributes, and experiences—you are likely to make incorrect decisions when affected by one of the seven fundamentals of failure, the negative variables. In this chapter and the next, you will be able to consider the most common fundamental of failure, human error, and see that it often springs from two other fundamentals of failure, incompetence and falsity. In this chapter, we see the collective errors of many people—often across generations—that lead to large, difficult-to-solve problems, such as Americans' shorter lives (more than four years shorter) compared with people in comparable countries. In the time it takes you to read the chapter, you will be able to determine whether your life span is likely to be longer or shorter than average, given the conditions under which you live.

Collective human errors and social ills produce a large amount of uncertainty and fear because you cannot make one decision that would eliminate the problems. For instance, we step into buses and airplanes because we presume that they are not defective and that the drivers and pilots will not make a mistake that leads to a fatal crash. We could focus exclusively on ensuring that airplane pilots are not incompetent. But, still, a pilot who possesses only average perception might not have the extraordinary perception needed to steer a plane to safety when a software error by an engineer years ago in the development of the plane causes an unanticipated, sharp, and uncontrollable descent.

If a pilot possesses average perceptual ability, then to avoid a crash after a steep descent, the pilot must compensate with at least one of the two other abilities (math or verbal), one of the four attributes (humility, empathy, fairness, or trust), or a large amount of experience (prior emergencies). For instance, the pilot might have the humility to recognize that his or her perception is only average and turn the flying over to the more qualified copilot. But the possibility of such a handoff in an emergency is not comforting or realistic.

This teaches that because such a late transfer of control from pilot to copilot might not prevent the plane from crashing, the software problem must be eliminated prior to takeoff. Such a preliminary analysis, describing how to account for average perception and prevent a crash, relying more on engineers who work on software than on pilots who fly planes, illustrates how the formula can be used to structure decision-making. You can see that a pilot's average abilities, attributes, and experience will sometimes be no match for the earlier incompetence, a fundamental of failure, by software engineers.

To prevent a crash, the airplane company's pilots must possess the positive variables, and someone in a different company, which employs the software engineers, must help to eliminate the fundamentals of failure that could overwhelm the pilots' positive variables. That we'll have several opportunities to protect ourselves before a crash occurs shows that big problems often emanate from incompetence among a lot of people. Unlike fate, however, where misfortune cannot be undone, an emergency usually means that someone who makes a correct decision can prevent additional harm. This means, fortunately, that even when almost everything has gone wrong, the presence of an emergency, by nature, means that you will have one final opportunity to make a correct decision to save yourself and possibly your company, family, or relationships from crashing.

Most daily events do not seem critical, and, through obedience or weariness, most people learn to accept incompetence and mediocrity and any number of other undesirable conditions. In considering how people view the world, a 2024 study examined 353,320 songs over fifty years in the five most popular music genres: rap, country, pop, rhythm and blues, and rock. The study found that the lyrics in the songs have become simpler, and more negative and personal. The researchers described similar findings of other studies of music lyrics: positive sentiments like joy and confidence have decreased, and negative sentiments (anger, disgust, or sadness) have increased. According to the researchers, "Words related to oneself ('me or mine') and words pointing to antisocial behavior ('hate' or 'kill') increased while words related to social interactions ('talk' or 'mate') and positive emotions ('love' or 'nice') decreased over time."[21]

Consider the words you hear each day in your environment, as well as the words you speak. The researchers found that the negative lyrics influence listeners, especially "where best-selling songs or artists are copied."[22] This finding is consistent with an increase in social polarization, which appears not to be an inherent personal characteristic but rather a consequence of negative interactions with other people. Similarly, other researchers found that "the data do not support the idea that affective polarization directly causes political violence" or "hate crimes."[23]

That means that negative lyrics in songs and violence do not inevitably grow from inside people. They arise through unpleasant interactions with each other. "Most violent acts that occur at political events or hate crimes are also likely spontaneous, impulsive decisions by individuals influenced by a crowd."[24] In other words, impressionable people should avoid troublemakers to avoid being lured into becoming troublemakers themselves.

One reason for what appears to be a lack of social consensus and personal happiness comes from the way Americans employ three sociopolitical divisions to make decisions and act on them: ethnicity, ideology, and religion.[25] These divisions have little or no relationship to reasoned decision-making, but they are often the basis for action. Other countries have one or two such divisions. As a result, America "stands out today as the only wealthy Western democracy with persistent levels of pernicious polarization," which divides "society into mutually antagonistic camps."[26]

The study on music lyrics found that romantic terms in songs did not change, but "sex-related aspects of relationships substantially increased." Perhaps as a result, today "rock listeners enjoy lyrics from older songs, while country fans prefer lyrics from new songs," which presumably are more positive than the lyrics in other genres. The smoothness or roughness of the road you're traveling on in the future might be indicated by the songs on your devices.[27]

THE CONSEQUENCES OF SOCIAL FAILURE ON YOU

Reflected in the harsh lyrics of songs, grim social conditions create small and large errors that are contagious. According to a report by the Citizens Budget Commission, a public interest group that monitors fiscal conditions, "Fare and toll evasion [in New York City] cost the Metropolitan Transportation Authority (MTA) approximately $1 billion in revenue in 2024."[28] On the subway, riders did not pay the fare on 10 percent of their rides. On the buses, where evasion is easier because buses do not have gates, riders did not pay fares on 44 percent of their two million daily bus rides.[29]

In the transportation system serving the Washington, DC region, nearly 70 percent of the bus riders did not pay their fares, the Transit Authority announced in 2024.[30] Stealing in plain sight, theft of services as it's called in New York, has become normal in many parts of America. If the $1 billion fare loss in New York City is allocated across its 8.4 million people, then each person pays $119 each year to neighbors who ride the buses without paying (though many of the residents are themselves the scofflaws).

By comparison, a report from 2019 found that the bus fare evasion rate was 11 percent in Paris, 5 percent in Toronto, and 1.5 percent in London.[31]

Perhaps for the first time, such social conditions have placed women in as much jeopardy as men. In a study from 2024, "researchers reported that younger women with anxiety or depression were nearly twice as likely to develop high blood pressure, high cholesterol or diabetes over a 10-year period compared with women who did not have these mental health conditions, putting them nearly on par with men of the same age in terms of heart disease risk."[32]

Women's alcohol use is especially costly. In 2022, researchers, to examine the effects of mothers' alcohol use on their children, including those in utero, used Social Security death files and Census Bureau records to calculate the number of deaths from 1975 to 2005. This period was when people born before and during

Prohibition (1920-1933) were expected to die. The study found that children born in dry counties during Prohibition, when alcohol was not prevalent, lived 1.7 years longer than children born in the same counties outside Prohibition, when alcohol was prevalent. The children of women who drink alcohol during pregnancy will not live as long as the children of women who do not drink during pregnancy.

The study noted that in the US today, "the share of women who drink during pregnancy has increased from 9.2% to 11.3% from 2011 to 2018. The associated problems, such as Fetal Alcohol Syndrome, impose an average lifetime cost of about $2 million per person."[33]

For 2024, US life expectancy at birth was 79.0 years (76.5 years for males and 81.4 years for females).[34] But that overall life expectancy was the lowest among comparable countries (Australia, Austria, Belgium, Canada, France, Germany, Japan, the Netherlands, Sweden, Switzerland, and the United Kingdom). For 2023, their average life expectancy was 82.5 years. The average per capita spending on health care in those countries was about $7,000, while in the US it was about $13,000.[35]

For nearly twice the money, Americans live 3.5 fewer years. That's partly because of the high homicide rate, which ranges from 2.9 to 26.5 times higher than in other countries. For 2017, the US homicide rate was 5.3 per 100,000 people. In Canada, France, the United Kingdom, Germany, Australia, New Zealand, South Korea, and Japan, respectively, the rates were 1.8, 1.3, 1.2, 1.0, 0.8, 0.7, 0.6, and 0.2. China's homicide rate was 0.6, making the US homicide rate 8.8 times higher than that of its most formidable rival.[36]

WHEN LEADERS FAIL

The Decision-Making Formula helps to explain generally why the US lags far behind peer countries on many measures. Some of the world's top performers in every endeavor reside in the US, making it appear that there are, at least collectively, people with significant math, verbal, and perceptual abilities and the attributes (humility, empathy, fairness, and trust) that allow them and their organizations to be enormously successful. But the high homicide rates and low life expectancy illustrate that the negative variables can overwhelm or exceed the positive variables. A different formula represents this concept:

> If negative variables > positive variables = incorrect decision-making.

Applied to your situation, whether in a job or a family, this shows how incorrect decision-making, often resulting in failure, can occur when the negative variables outweigh the many positive variables you've worked a lifetime to develop.

One of the negative variables—that is, one of the fundamentals of failure—is incompetence, which is embodied by people who hold positions for which they are not qualified. NASA, though one of the most prominent federal agencies, lost the shuttles Challenger and Columbia and fourteen astronauts in two infamous missions, seven on each shuttle flight. In 1986, Challenger's O-ring seals, in cold weather in Florida, became rigid and could not seal joints on the shuttle. On devices and other machines, an O-ring prevents fluids and gases from escaping from connectors, such as tubes. A warm, supple O-ring, like moist bread dough, can adhere to a surface and seal the area where the tubes or other connectors meet. But a cold, hard O-ring, like a frozen slice of bread, might not provide a seal, allowing gases to rush through a pinpoint opening. Seventy-three seconds into Challenger's flight, hot exhaust rushed through a leak and burned a hole in an external fuel tank, which exploded.[37] Aerodynamic forces destroyed the shuttle.[38]

NASA had decided to launch Challenger after the nighttime temperatures had plunged to record cold in Florida, twenty-four to twenty-six degrees, freezing the O-rings. At the time of the launch, the temperature was thirty-six degrees. Just before the explosion, a CNN commentator summarized the pressure that led to NASA's incorrect decision to launch. "The twenty-fifth space shuttle mission is now on the way after more delays than NASA cares to count. This morning it looked as though they were not going to be able to get off." One second later, Challenger's fuel tank exploded.[39]

In 2003, during the shuttle Columbia's ascent, 81.7 seconds after liftoff, insulation foam, the size of a briefcase, dislodged from an external fuel tank. It struck one or two protective carbon tiles that shielded its left wing. Ground cameras showed small debris spurting from the area of the strike like water sprinkling from a shower head. On at least six prior shuttle flights, most recently four months earlier on the shuttle Atlantis, insulation foam had dislodged from a fuel tank; one tank was damaged. (During the shuttle program, from 1981 to 2011, the fuel tanks, after lifting the shuttles toward space, were jettisoned from the shuttles and fell into the ocean, where they were recovered.) After the launch, NASA managers underestimated the possible danger lurking in Columbia's left wing.

Concluding that the risk to the shuttle was small, the managers informed the astronauts obliquely of the foam strike but reassured them that it presented little or no danger. Regardless of the risk, the NASA managers believed that no benefit would come from informing the astronauts of their extensive internal discussions about the foam strike. That silence, alone, the concealment of possible end-of-life information, illustrated in NASA's leaders a significant misunderstanding of the human condition and a general lack of judgment. Most people would want to know the end is near and have a few minutes to speak with their most important people before they die.

In another misjudgment, NASA's managers, to avoid embarrassment, rejected asking the US military to use its spy satellites to photograph the part of Columbia's left wing that the astronauts and cameras could not see, the one or two carbon tiles that had been struck. After the foam strike, a NASA engineer, Rodney Rocha, recognized the danger and, on behalf of thirty other NASA engineers, pleaded with managers to ask the Defense Department to use its satellites or to ask other agencies to use their powerful ground telescopes to photograph or observe the left wing. Rocha made at least six requests, and other engineers made two requests. But Linda Ham, the chair of the mission management team, cancelled the requests.

"All were turned aside," according to a *New York Times* report. One manager said he would not be "Chicken Little."

In an email, the flight director, LeRoy Cain, wrote, "I consider it to be a dead issue."

The *Times* report, from September 2003—after the completion of the official report on the Columbia disaster by an investigative board in August 2003—concluded, "The new information makes it clear that the failure to follow up on the request for outside imagery, the first step in discovering the damage and perhaps mounting a rescue effort, did not simply fall through bureaucratic cracks but was actively, even hotly resisted by mission managers."[40]

After its fifteen-day mission, Columbia and its astronauts descended. During reentry, hot gases penetrated the damaged heat shield and, over several minutes, the gases presumably melted the inner core of the left wing until its superstructure crumbled. This led to Columbia's disintegration into an uncountable number of pieces, which dropped onto rural areas in Texas.[41]

NASA's failure to correct the flying-foam problem prior to Columbia's mission and its misjudgment in launching Challenger led to incalculable human suffering among the families of the astronauts and, most tragically, the astronauts themselves. After the explosion of Challenger's fuel tank over the Atlantic, the shuttle's capsule survived. The astronauts remained alive. From the acceleration that was already in motion prior to the explosion, the capsule rose for an additional twenty seconds.

The capsule then stopped at its apogee, its highest point, for an infinitesimal moment. Though communication with the astronauts was lost, data showed that, at some time after the explosion, Challenger's two pilots tried to fly the capsule, but to no avail. At least three astronauts switched on auxiliary oxygen. Their capsule dropped twelve miles, toward the ocean, reaching a terminal velocity of two hundred miles per hour. The harrowing, uncontrolled descent of the astronauts, apparently all of them alive, took two minutes. And then their capsule crashed into the Atlantic Ocean, a collision that caused them to die.

The shuttle Columbia disintegrated forty miles above the surface of the Earth. Its astronauts suffered one of three agonizing causes of death. Their depressurized capsule might have led to gases forming in the astronauts' bodies and creating bubbles in their blood vessels. Bubbles in blood vessels block the flow of blood, which leads to strokes and then death.

In another alternative, the astronauts might have died from flying debris striking them inside the capsule.

The final alternative, likely for some of the astronauts, is that they died when colliding with the ground, after falling through the air during the final forty miles.

Parts of the remains of all fourteen astronauts were found on the sea floor and in the rural areas of Texas. The final cause of their deaths, their bodies striking the water or ground, helps to emphasize two cultural conditions that led to failure at NASA. Of course, a *cultural condition* simply emanates from individuals who make errors, from incompetence. The conditions were poor communication within NASA and the "normalization of deviance." NASA's leaders accepted substandard conditions and minimized the risks from rigid O-rings and flying insulation foam.

The poor communication represents a restriction on speaking, which is one of the most debilitating fundamentals of failure. Discouraging expression and dissent, NASA had adopted a command structure like that of the US military. One of the investigators of the Challenger disaster wrote in 2024 about the problems with NASA's lack of communication stemming from its mimicry of the military:

> As former CAIB [Columbia Accident Investigation Board] member Scott Hubbard has noted, human spaceflight at that time was a very hierarchical operation, with deep roots in military culture, with orders coming from on high. It was also very procedures-based. Things outside of normal procedures, like seeking new data on the debris strike, could be shut down by orders from senior personnel in the shuttle program.

The investigator, Dwayne A. Day, found that NASA, when confronted with error, showed "a lack of curiosity within the program when the shuttle did not perform the way it was supposed to."

Day wrote, "I distinctly remember one NASA shuttle tile expert, one of the people who had developed them in the early 1970s, who was full of blustery confidence about how shuttle tiles were tough and not easily damaged. He was not merely being defensive: he was clearly not interested in *how* they could be damaged."[42]

Why, then, despite believing they have critical information to share, do people remain silent? In a documentary film from 2024, Rodney Rocha, the prescient engineer who pleaded with NASA's management to request satellite photos of Columbia's damaged left wing, expressed disappointment in himself for not complaining directly to top leaders. Somewhat defensively, as a reason for not speaking more loudly, and he spoke more than anyone, Rocha explained how the military-like, hierarchical structure of NASA prevented him from going over the heads of his managers. Of course, there were no prison bars that stopped him, but like many others, indeed, almost everyone, Rocha feared being demoted to a position he did not like or losing his job.

In November 2024, a British consulting group, Hesper, tried to explain why Rocha was deterred from contacting top managers and administrators:

> Rocha later explained…"*I just couldn't do it* [speak up in the meeting about the foam risk]. She [his senior manager] *was way up here* [gestures with hand overhead] *and I was way down here* [gestures with low hand]…." The organisational culture at NASA emphasized hierarchy, and a strict adherence to the chain of command; the culture made it

> challenging for lower-level employees to question or contradict their superiors even when they had legitimate safety concerns.[43]

Hesper applied the same analysis to the Challenger disaster, seventeen years earlier, finding that "hierarchical reporting relations" prevented candid discussions.[44]

NASA appears not to have corrected its systems. In June 2024, NASA and the Boeing Company, after years of delays, launched the Starliner, a ship designed to take astronauts to the International Space Station. Immediately after launch, the vessel experienced helium leaks and the loss of five of twenty-eight thrusters. A Boeing official said, "Now that we're in flight and we've seen a couple more leaks, if it is a common cause across those flanges [plates that increase the strength of the connection between two objects], then there might be something more to the flange itself, maybe a bad lot of seals or some other variable."[45] In March 2025, NASA's other spacecraft contractor, SpaceX, returned the astronauts safely to Earth, more than nine months late.

EFFECTIVE ACTION IN AN EMERGENCY: ADAPTABILITY AND FLEXIBILITY

With your knowledge of the origins of such large-scale failures, whether the shuttle disasters or low life expectancy in the US, you can be assured that you have the capacity to solve the most difficult problems if you are open-minded and adaptive. The narrow-minded, hierarchical operations at NASA contributed to the loss of the shuttles and their crews. Unlike businesses, NASA did not have any competitors. Other than bureaucracy, NASA faced no outside threats but still failed because its managers introduced the fundamentals of failure into its operations—silence, fear, inaction, incompetence, and human error.

In contrast, the people of Ukraine were confronted by an enemy who wanted to destroy them, but they survived. On February 24, 2022, Russia invaded Ukraine, where the disbelieving citizens had little time for reflection or planning for war. A nation of 38 million people might not be expected to last long against Russia, with 144 million people, the fourth largest army in the world, and nuclear weapons. But the Ukrainians learned quickly how to survive, and the lessons are applicable to the resolution of your personal and professional issues.

The Ukrainians, while dependent on Western aid and weaponry, saved their country by employing three mental approaches: adaptability, flexibility, and rapid decision-making. More than two years after the beginning of the war, in April 2024, on a goodwill tour, Ukrainian military officers, who were then assigned to teach at the National Defense University of Ukraine, lectured to military audiences in the US on how to survive against a superior force, and I attended one of their two-day seminars. Recognizing the Russian army's strengths, the Ukrainian officers described how successful responses, albeit with losses, can be formulated quickly.

In the moments leading up to the war, the Ukrainians, to disguise their last-minute defense preparations, pretended not to believe the Russians would invade. They misled the Russians by leaving their few aircraft at known bases. But ten minutes after the Russians began the onslaught on a course, by then known to the Ukrainians, they flew their planes to safety in western Ukraine, opposite the invaders from the north and east.

On a narrow road leading into Ukraine, the Russians massed a sixty-mile-long convoy of armaments and supplies. With limited weaponry, the Ukrainians attacked the front and middle of the convoy, halting the Russian advance and inhibiting a retreat. Unable to move forward or turn around because of destroyed vehicles and impassible ground on the sides of the road, the Russians and their vehicles were temporarily stalled.

> The lesson the Ukrainian officers taught was to rely on humility, one of the positive attributes (HEFT), which for them was a recognition of their limitations. They did not exaggerate their individual abilities or the ability of their army or the Ukrainian people to prevail over Russia. The Ukrainian officers repeatedly emphasized that success depends on adaptability and flexibility. Indeed, a Harvard Business School professor, Joseph Fuller, concluded at the same time that the most important leadership skill is adaptability. Fuller found that "what sets high achievers apart from everyone else...isn't their confidence or business acumen—it's their adaptability." Fuller found, "They're not wedded to some predetermined career path that they set when they were a student or starting their first job. They're open to unexpected opportunities and embrace change instead of fearing it."[46]

Adaptability to the Ukrainians, in war, meant that their actions should follow quickly from their decisions. The Ukrainian officers explained that they had a vibrant corps of noncommissioned officers, essentially middle management, who were authorized and capable of making decisions on the ground and while on the run. Previously enlisted soldiers, these NCOs provide a communications and operational link between officers and the enlisted or conscripted soldiers. In contrast, the Russian army, like its predecessor Soviet army, does not have NCOs and is notoriously less adaptable, more reliant on sending masses of soldiers into a battle, and more willing than other armies to sacrifice them.

The Ukrainians made seemingly basic changes in their training and emphasized the need to do so quickly. They recommended the following modifications, which are applicable to many organizations:

- Teach and learn exclusively what is necessary.
- Shorten training programs.
- Use mobile training centers.
- Give noncommissioned officers more discretion.
- Learn to use technology.
- Recognize that teachers are crucial to performance.
- Recognize that training and education should not stop.

For example, in 2025, Stephen Bryen, a former US deputy undersecretary of defense, lauded the Ukrainians' use of inexpensive shotgun drones against Russian Mavics, which are drones that drop grenades on the Ukrainians. The Ukrainians learned how to maneuver their own drones to shoot blasts of pellets, like an unmanned shotgun in the sky, at the Mavics and destroy them.[47]

Relishing the method, the Ukrainians, recognizing that drones are like darting birds, used propeller planes from World War I to chase and destroy the Russian drones, which can fly about 115 miles an hour, while the planes can fly faster, up to 180 miles an hour. When the plane's pilot closes in on the drones, another soldier opens a sliding glass canopy and, with a shotgun, shoots at the Russian drones.[48]

However, as the brutal war continued, with no end in sight, the Ukrainians realized that the training they had received from Western militaries had been inadequate. The director of the American Enterprise Institute's Critical Threats Project, Fred Kagan, in 2024, described the limits on the training the Ukrainians had received. "It's now clear that the NATO trainers helping prepare Ukrainian forces to fight did not really understand the war as it was being fought and did not internalize the challenges that Ukrainian troops would face trying rapidly to learn how to use Western systems and apply NATO doctrine without having the full panoply of NATO capabilities on which NATO militaries would have relied."[49]

In other words, you can't change course effectively unless you've developed skills previously in the area where your issue or problem resides. In the war, the consequences of a lack of deep knowledge surfaced in late 2025, when Ukraine's generals, who had been trained in Soviet doctrine, inhibited their soldiers' creativity. "Three years on, Ukraine's military has slipped back into a more rigid, top-down mode of fighting with roots in the Soviet era, creating mounting frustration about unnecessary casualties while hurting civilian morale and army recruitment. Without overhauls, the Soviet-style habits could undermine Ukraine's ability to sustain its defense against Russia, which shows no sign of relenting in its quest to conquer the country," according to a report in the *Wall Street Journal*.[50]

In essence, this is a message to everyone that micromanagement is destructive, often deadly. To project aggressiveness, the Ukrainian generals instituted a centralized command culture, dictated how to fight battles, ordered assaults that had little chance of success, and sacrificed soldiers for no tactical or strategic reason. Albeit usually not including death, that description is reminiscent of failing businesses and organizations. The complaints of the Ukrainian soldiers mirrored the seven fundamentals of failure, especially fear. One soldier complained of "stupid orders" and generals who are "only capable of reprimands, investigations, imposing penalties."[51]

Despite the enormous population and resource advantages of the Russians, the war, after more than four years, remained a stalemate, with only death on each side to signify the other nation's success. In war, indeed in every endeavor, success does not necessarily follow from great resources. The US and its military failed or lost in the last four wars, all against impoverished countries (North Korea, Vietnam, Afghanistan, and Iraq). A complete evaluation of the US-Iran war, which started in 2026, will depend on whether, in future years, Iran continues or ceases trying to develop nuclear weapons. Among seven industrialized and allied nations, the G7 (Canada, France, Germany, Italy, Japan, and the UK), the US in 2023 was last in confidence in national institutions (military, judicial, national government, and honesty of elections), at 49 percent, behind Canada's leading 65 percent.[52] Americans' pessimism may be well-grounded. In 2023, the US was first (which means worst) in people reporting hunger. In the US, 26 percent of the respondents in a poll answered affirmatively to the following question: "Have there been times in the past 12 months when you did not have enough money to buy food that you or your family needed?" The percentages for the other countries ranged from 6 percent (Japan) to 17 percent (Canada).[53]

Why do hunger, high homicide rates, and low life expectancy plague the US more than they do other comparable countries? In this chapter, you began to see that, despite Americans' significant abilities, attributes, and experiences, which are the positive variables in the Decision-Making Formula, good conditions inside the US can be overwhelmed by the fundamentals of failure. This illustrates that no matter how hard you work to develop and how much you contribute to your employer and family, you must try to avoid the conditions and people who bring failure to your doorstep, whether the managers at NASA, the Russians in Ukraine, or the dangerous characters in the next chapter who might be masquerading as your friends.

Key Points

- Positive variables > negative variables = correct decision-making.
- Adaptability, flexibility, and speedy decision-making are critical to success.
- Human error springs from incompetence.
- Pursue jobs and positions for which you are fit.
- Associate with people who want you to succeed.

CHAPTER 2

THE MAFIA OF IRREDEEMABLE PEOPLE

(RESPONDING TO THOSE WHO HURT YOU)

Many people are unprepared for adversity because they underestimate how much pain other people can inflict on them. The people who hurt you usually do so unintentionally, but when they do it intentionally the moral injury you feel or harm you experience from the shock that someone would do this is in an undesirable category all its own. To learn to recognize when you are about to be hurt and, better, how to prevent harm in the first place, the case study in this chapter introduces some of the most aberrant and casually uncaring people anyone could encounter. Through them, you'll learn that the primary reason why their intentional wrongdoing is surprising is that we've been fooled by their falsity, one of the fundamentals of failure, their ability to present a persona that is not true to their nature, and we'll see how, as a result, individuals around them make astonishing errors.

After learning about their nefarious deeds, your challenge will be to identify which people around you are not concerned with your well-being or, worse, would act to hurt you for some reason or for no reason. If you find them, you should respond to protect yourself or, if that's not possible, move away from them.

The first character in the case is probably America's most notorious police detective. He worked for the New York City Police Department when homicides in the city were at an all-time high, exceeding 2,000 each year and peaking at 2,262 in 1990 (but now down to three to four hundred yearly).[54] He contributed to the death toll. The detective, Louis Eppolito, whom I was assigned to work with before the depth of his wrongdoing became known, moonlighted as an assassin for the Mafia, the Lucchese family, and helped to kill at least eight people.[55]

Through Detective Eppolito, you'll consider whether people who try intentionally to harm you might change their ways in the future. Realistically, whether in business or relationships, the answer is *no*. Eppolito and his accomplices once mistakenly killed a man because his name was identical to the name of their target. Undeterred, they went on to kill again. Though most people will not interact with the Mafia, the killing of the innocent man teaches that you must be aware of your surroundings and, especially, the people with whom you interact the most.

In applying the Decision-Making Formula to this case, you'll see, in Eppolito's and the other characters' behavior, what appears to be the most extraordinary human errors. You might initially believe their errors are the worst because of the terrible consequences that resulted, the deaths of many people. However, do not be misdirected by thinking that their desire to harm other people is somehow limited to them. If you think about the competitors that you've encountered and the people with whom you've worked every day, as well as those closest to you professionally and personally, the structure of the harm that they intentionally administered is the same as that employed by Eppolito and his cronies. Though their results were more devastating, the harm brought to you by other people is often as long-lasting emotionally or financially.

To make this point more concrete, recall the positive variables—your abilities, attributes, and observations or experiences. In the workplace, remember whether someone has acted to harm your interests despite your good work. Some people, like supervisors, have done this merely to assert their control over you and obtain self-satisfaction, with no economic or material benefit to the business or organization. In other instances, a fellow employee might have undermined you to obtain a position or additional rewards, money, or advancement that otherwise would have been yours, or maybe he did it to hurt you without regard to his benefit.

Concerning the people who are closest to you, perhaps after a dispute, how many of them have not answered or returned your telephone call while they knew that their non-response would make you worry or experience distress? If a person tried to hurt you by making you feel alone or isolated, you'll remember the experience, especially if it was part of the deterioration of a relationship. That's because, and it bears repeating, experiencing intentional harm from another person is in a category of hurt unlike all others, and when you anticipate or feel this you should know to exercise keen vigilance to protect your interests.

To learn to deal with the harm you might receive from others, apply the Decision-Making Formula to the conditions in your life. First, consider what positive variable will be most beneficial to you. Though you always need your abilities and attributes, your most useful positive variable in the case ahead will be your observations of other people. You probably know from experience who is most likely to be the culprit who will hurt you. Second, watch how Detective Eppolito and the other characters casually harmed other people. Through observing them, anticipate how and when in the future someone who is uncaring could try to harm you.

Next, recognize that it is nearly a fixed principle in the universe that you will find it very difficult to speak up or act in response to those who have greater authority or on whom you depend financially or emotionally. There are innumerable justifications for remaining silent while on the job or in a relationship. But speaking or acting becomes easier when you know you need to do it to protect yourself or members of your family.

The lesson in the story ahead is that you should almost always reject silence and inaction when someone tries to hurt you because that person, friend or foe, if the opportunity arises again, will probably try to inflict harm again. If either speaking or acting does not seem feasible, you should then recognize that the only other alternatives are to leave the job or situation or stay in place and remain silent. In sum, when someone intentionally hurts you, all your responses, including silence, will be emotionally wrenching.

DETERMINING RESPONSIBILITY: WHO IS MOST LIKELY TO HURT YOU?

To know when to speak up or act or respond in some way, you should first know how to identify who exhibits culpable or blameworthy behavior. At one extreme, an infant who flails her chubby arms and hits her mother in the face did not think about hurting anyone and would not be responsible for making her mother feel slight pain. But you want to find a more methodical way to assess who is responsible, which will help you determine whether and how to act. Begin by answering what seems to be an elementary question. Do I believe that everybody should be treated the same for doing the same act?

Almost everyone has been conditioned to answer *yes*, but the better answer is *no*. To see why, assume that in downtown Highland Falls, three automobile drivers, on different days, drive their cars in the same manner, at twenty-five miles per hour, over three pedestrians in the same crosswalk. After being struck by the cars, each pedestrian dies. Should the local prosecutor bring the same criminal homicide charge, if any, against each driver because each of them committed the same act? *No*.

The reason why different charges should be brought is that in evaluating people you should consider not only their actions but also the thinking that accompanies their actions. Assume that the first driver was a hitman who killed the pedestrian in exchange for money. The second driver was a teenager who, without driver's training, stole a car and did not care whether he drove it without prior training. The third driver was an elderly person who could not hear or see well, perhaps slouching so low she needed to peer up and through the steering wheel to glimpse the road. She did not realize she should not drive an automobile and did not see the pedestrian.

With those few additional facts, you will now conclude that the level of blame and amount of punishment that you will attach to each of the drivers should be based primarily on their mental states, not on their action. The mental states of the drivers, combined with the action (running over a pedestrian) and the result (death of a pedestrian), provide the structure of human error.

The third element, the result, is important to know because a hitman, despite wanting to kill a pedestrian and running over her with his automobile, will receive less punishment if, for some reason, perhaps prompt medical care, the pedestrian does not die from the collision with the car. This leads to identifying the mental states that make people most responsible or deserving of blame:

- Intent (wanting an act to cause a result) (hitman).
- Recklessness (not caring if an act causes a result) (teenager).
- Negligence (not knowing an act could cause a result) (elderly person).

This structure helps you see that because you do not have enough time to prevent all infractions and some infractions cause little or no harm, you should expend the greatest effort and most time to address (1) intentional harm that is connected with (2) an act that can cause (3) the most harmful result.

To illustrate this point, consider the decision-making of the most senior army officer at the US Military Academy, which over the past two hundred and twenty-four years has educated America's most prominent generals. In July 2025, Lieutenant General Steven Gilland, the superintendent, addressed new faculty members, who were lower-ranking captains and majors that had recently obtained master's degrees that allowed them to teach at West Point. In a monologue, Gilland explained the importance of his work by describing how he believed the academy was a superior institution:

> We are not a college, and we are not a university. We're a hell of a lot more than that and our nation expects more from us.... You better believe I'm serious about it.... [Our job is to] make people better human beings...[and] we're serious about this.

That's taking on a lot of responsibility, making a lot of people better human beings. To achieve this goal, making people better, Gilland warned the officers: "I care about what you are doing, saying, or acting."

Gilland then emphasized the importance of conformity, dressed up as standards. "I need your help…in settin' the standard," he told the officers. "The U.S. Army and the U.S. Military Academy is (sic) a standard based institution. The standards are not that challenging. Basic things."

Gilland then used examples of standard-based behavior. He pointed at an officer in the audience who had little or no hair. "Major Jones, you clearly don't have a problem of meeting the standard for a haircut." Some officers laughed nervously.

Gilland was more serious. "Some of you do. And you know what? That's a problem."

Gilland then became more specific. "The standard of appearance…the standard of our language, and we talk about our language. Hey, guess what, you don't walk and talk on your [cell] phone [which is a rule at West Point]. Do ya? Ya all know that. And believe me. This is what you're gonna get from Gilland."

He asked the officers, "Why do you do it?"

An obedient officer who was looking for praise raised his hand and answered. "Sir, it's an issue of character."

"Right on," said Gilland.

Gilland introduced the command sergeant major, the highest-ranking enlisted soldier at West Point, Phil K. Barretto, to help Gilland emphasize appearances. Addressing the officers, Barretto emphasized the importance of wearing authorized socks when exercising. The socks must be black and cover the ankle bone. Barretto explained why:

> Black socks. It ain't about the socks. If you think it's about the socks you miss the message. It's not about the socks.... And the standard, and enforcing the standard. On time. It's never about the socks people...because there's something else that can happen other than the damn PT [physical training] socks.... No show socks.... And we made him go back to his room and go get the right socks.... He turned around. He got the right socks.

All organizations need some uniformity to show that they are cohesive and the people inside them respect each other, but we should consider whether the standard that receives the most time or greatest emphasis in an important meeting is sock wearing.

Gilland's and Barretto's emphasis on correct haircuts, telephone usage, speaking, and socks requires officers to spend time worrying about and fearing punishment for insignificant infractions. That meeting wasn't the end of the issue surrounding socks. Two weeks later, in the first meeting of the 2025–2026 academic year for all instructors, the vice dean and number two person in the Dean's Office, Colonel Krista Watts, welcomed everyone this way, with her first words:

> Ladies and gentlemen, and welcome back. And I hope everyone has had a great summer. And before we start I have an administrative announcement. We really need your help in adhering to uniform regulations. Specifically...for military who are conducting physical training.... The regulation is... you have to be at the correct APFU [army physical fitness uniform] and we seem to get this wrong.

> The correct APFU, check your socks, that seems to be a common place that we get this wrong, no ear buds.... Anyone here can make the correction. If you see somebody doing something wrong, just make the correction.

Next up in the same meeting and following Watts was the academic dean, Brigadier General Shane Reeves. Not explaining how teachers can function without providing their opinions to students, he directed all the faculty members to do just that, to keep their opinions to themselves. In providing what the military calls guidance, the opinions of higher-ranking officers ironically, Reeves explained: "If you start to feel that perhaps maybe you're starting to advocate for a particular position or ideology, which I don't think you do, when you're taking a position where you're like why we believe this, so I'll help the Cadets believe this way, you're wrong. That's not what we do. They don't need to know what I believe."

These senior officers' warnings were effective and produced 100 percent sock compliance, and there's a benefit to attending to small things, in that habitual behavior can teach and remind people to attend to more important matters. But the connection between wearing conforming socks and winning a war is so tenuous and distant that everyone subject to perpetual punishment and embarrassment for wearing non-conforming socks will be unlikely to rely on the judgment of the person who is fixated on the socks.

Through the Decision-Making Formula, consider where conformity leads:

> If (natural abilities + attributes of success) + (observations/practices) > (fundamentals of failure) = correct decision-making.

For every set of parentheses indicating the positive variables, see below the downward arrows, which indicate how conformity depletes the positive variables (abilities, attributes, and observations/practices). Then see the upward arrow in the space for the negative variables (the seven fundamentals of failure). Conformity enhances the negative variables. In this scenario, we can reconfigure the formula to express the failure that ensues from needless conformity:

$$\text{If} (\downarrow + \downarrow) + (\downarrow) > (\uparrow) = \text{incorrect decision-making.}$$

In this scenario, with the positive variables down and the negative variables up, the positive variables would likely not be greater than the negative variables. Thus, a resulting decision (on the right side of the = sign) would be incorrect.

High-ranking people in organizations pass their thinking to everyone else. Soon after Gilland emphasized conforming socks, a cadet studying a legal case considered whether someone who steals a small item from a dark location should be responsible for unintentionally burning down a structure after lighting a match to see better. In thinking about whether the thief should be responsible for arson, the cadet explained how a colonel had seen the cadet running with socks that showed the manufacturer's logo at ankle-bone level, which is a sock violation.

The colonel ordered the offending cadet to his office to explain to him the reasons why cadets should wear conforming socks. The colonel said his best friend had been killed in a helicopter crash during the war in Afghanistan because "one screw was loose" on the helicopter. That tells you, cadet, to focus on small things, said the colonel. The enforcement of the rules regarding foot gear expanded, and during that time, the academic year of 2025-2026, many military instructors, before they began teaching a class, required a designated cadet to inspect the clothes, especially the shoes, of all the other cadets. Once during an inspection, the instructor explained to a visiting military officer who was observing the class, "We're building skills, not judgment."

On hearing the colonel's helicopter story, though sad, it's fair to question his assessment by wondering how anyone in a war zone observing helicopter wreckage could know how one screw, or which screw, caused a crash. Though anyone can empathize with the colonel's grief, his one-screw theory, even if correct, is so unlikely to be confirmed, given the wreckage, that many cadets and officers who hear the colonel's conclusion about socks will be more likely to question his judgment and disregard important points he might make in the future.

> On hearing the recitation of the colonel's one-screw theory as justification for wearing conforming socks, another student in the class, who had been previously befuddled by the sock rule, said that good leaders know to spend more time on helicopter maintenance and less time on ensuring that everyone wears conforming socks.

Nonetheless, keep an open mind and try to use a logical structure to measure the value of wearing conforming socks. In other words, what will help you decide how to spend your time? By way of analogy, consider driver A, who, in Highland Falls, without stopping completely, drives his car slowly through a stop sign. This causes driver B to swerve her car away from driver A's car. There's no collision, but B's swerving her car and the loss of speed delay her journey by ten seconds.

Driver B continues down the road and enters the scenic Palisades Parkway, a divided two-lane highway in each direction. Twenty minutes later, B approaches an entrance ramp on her right side, where cars can merge into her lane. Driver C merges into B's lane. But driver C misjudges the distance between C's car and B's car. C drives his car into the right rear bumper of B's car, causing it to roll over and over, and B dies.

Did driver A's rolling through the stop sign twenty minutes earlier back in Highland Falls contribute to B's death later on the Palisades Parkway? It's possible, in the way it's also possible that many other events earlier that day, such as someone cutting in line in front of B at a donut shop and delaying B, led to B's collision with C at the fatal moment. The line cutter and driver A, however, could not have foreseen that their actions would contribute to B's death and would not be legally, and probably not morally, responsible.

This scenario shows that, with a decision-making model, you can better recognize the important matters that might contribute to significant problems and the lesser events that do not require an expenditure of your time. If logic (perhaps based on cost-benefit, utilitarian principles) tells you that driver A, who rolled through the stop sign, should not be responsible for the death of driver B, then you will be far more certain that a cadet or military officer who wears non-conforming socks would be far less likely to be responsible for a helicopter crash years later during a war. Few leaders who could ensure 100 percent compliance with a rule, as Lieutenant General Gilland can through punishing officers and cadets who do not comply, would expend their leadership capital on forcing people to wear conforming socks.

DETECTIVE LOUIS EPPOLITO: HOW IS HE DIFFERENT?

While on one of my two weekly twenty-four-hour shifts required of new prosecutors for about six months, a dispatcher for the District Attorney's office in Brooklyn, on November 4, 1986, directed me to the 63rd police precinct, just off Flatbush Avenue, to help Detective Louis Eppolito interview a witness in the strangulation killing of a woman. My job was to help the NYPD investigate some of the most serious human errors: murders, rapes, kidnappings, and arsons.

I arrived at the precinct to find a twenty-seven-year-old marine who had contacted police to report that he had jogged past a parked car with a man in the driver's seat and a woman in the front passenger seat. The marine ran ahead and later turned around and jogged back along the same route. When he neared the car the second time, he saw the man in the driver's seat walk around the front of the car and pull the woman, or at least her body, from the passenger seat. The man, wearing red pants and a plaid shirt, looked up and spotted the marine, but, after dropping her body on the ground, he got back into his car and drove away.

The marine ran to the corpse and then to a nearby business to call the police. When officers arrived at the scene, the woman was on the ground, dead from ligature strangulation, meaning something like a rope had been wound around her neck, and the police found a rope near her body. From the woman's apparent lack of medical care, detectives believed, correctly as it turned out, that she had worked in the sex trade. Naturally, her clients should be interviewed, and that's what led them to the suspect, Barry Gibbs.

Ten days later, coincidentally, I was working another twenty-four-hour shift and was directed again to meet Detective Eppolito. He had a suspect, Gibbs, who generally matched the marine's description of the man who dropped the body. Eppolito asked me to help conduct a lineup in which the marine would view Gibbs and five other people, known as fillers, who stand or sit in a line. In a room with a one-way mirror, the marine identified Gibbs as the man who "took the body out of the car." That's a sobering moment because the later testimony of one witness in court is legally sufficient to find a suspect guilty of any crime (except treason), from petty theft to a killing that is punishable with the death penalty.[56]

After the lineup, Mr. Gibbs said he wanted to speak with me, and, in an office with Eppolito and another detective present, a technician recorded our conversation, which lasted about nine minutes. After waiving his right to remain silent, Gibbs said, "They [detectives] can investigate anything they want to show that I'm innocent. That's what I'd like them to prove.... I normally do the same thing.... I have no car. [On the day of the killing] I went downstairs, ate at Continental Caterers, went upstairs, took a shower, got ready for work and went to work at five o'clock."

In the second half of the interview, Mr. Gibbs provided surprising answers after I asked whether he knew the deceased woman.

> Q. Do you have or own a pair of red pants?
>
> A. Yes, I do.
>
> Q. Do you have or own a plaid shirt?
>
> A. Yes, I do.
>
> Q. Alright. You understand that we're investigating a homicide that occurred?
>
> A. Yes, I do.
>
> Q. Do you know the name of the person who was killed?

A. Not at all.

Q. If I, I told you that the name of the person that was killed was named Virginia Robertson, do you know her?

A. No.

Q. Had you ever seen anybody by that name?

A. No, not until the Detective showed me a picture.

Q. I understand. Had you ever talked with anybody named Virginia Robertson.

Q. Not at all.

A. Had you ever gone to any social gatherings with anyone named Virginia Robertson?

A. Not at all. Only to drop her off in my car one day and that was it.

Q. Drop, you dropped who off in your car?

A. I dropped her off in my car one day. I had met her on the street, alright—

Q. Met who on the street?

A. This, supposedly—the deceased.

Q. Uh, huh.

A. And she came up my house, she, she was a crack addict. We done crack together.

Q. Do you remember what day that you met her?

A. I met her some time last year.

Q. About what, about when?

A. March, maybe.

Q. Uh, huh. And how many times did you see her in the, in the last year since that—

A. I haven't seen that girl, other than maybe on three or four different occasions. And the last time I saw this girl was the end of August, beginning of September. And it was briefly, on the street—

Q. And that—

A. She rang my doorbell.

Q. Uh, huh.

A. I told her to get lost. And that was the last I saw her.

Q. And that was Virginia Robertson?

A. I don't know the name.

Q. You mentioned that you have some red pants and plaid shirt. It might be helpful to this investigation to get those red pants and plaid shirt—would you have any objection to me, or a Police Officer—

A. Not at all—

> Q. Getting those—would you have any objection to our going to your apartment to get those?
>
> A. Not at all.
>
> Q. Would you give us the keys to go get those?
>
> A. I certainly will.
>
> Q. Do you know where, where Virginia Robertson lived?
>
> A. No. I remember dropping her off on Foster Avenue one time—Foster, one block before Ocean Avenue.

Those are the kinds of responses provided by people under stress. Gibbs had steadfastly maintained his innocence, but, after denying four times that he knew the woman, he felt compelled to explain his relationship with her.

A different assistant district attorney handled the case at trial, and the most significant additional evidence came from a cellmate who was in jail with Gibbs prior to the trial. He testified that Gibbs said he killed the woman because she tried to steal from him. The jury found Gibbs guilty of murder, and the judge sentenced him to life in prison, with parole possible after twenty years. Over the next decade, Mr. Gibbs appealed the conviction through state and federal courts and lost each time.

HOW TO KNOW WHO WILL HURT YOU

Nineteen years after the killing, however, the District Attorney's Office asked a judge to vacate Barry Gibbs's conviction and release him because a new cooperating witness in a federal case, a drug dealer named Burton Kaplan, implicated Detective Eppolito and his partner, Stephen Caracappa, in at least eight killings on behalf of the Mafia. Kaplan had been imprisoned in the 1980s with a man named Frank Santoro. Santoro was a small-time mobster who had a loose connection to the Gambino crime family, one of the five Mafia families in New York City (Bonanno, Columbo, Genovese, and Lucchese). In plotting how to make money once released from prison, Santoro told Kaplan that his cousin was a police detective. The cousin, Eppolito, and his partner, Steven Caracappa, would become known as the Mafia Cops. In 1986, they, according to Kaplan's later testimony, entered a murderous alliance with the Lucchese family to kill various adversaries within organized crime, a conspiracy that led to the eight deaths.

Though suspected by the NYPD's Internal Affairs Bureau of having Mafia ties, Eppolito retired from the department unscathed in 1990, at age forty-two. Almost humorously, Eppolito, in 1992, wrote a book, *Mafia Cop: The Story of an Honest Cop Whose Family Was the Mob.*[57] In almost a dozen movies, including *Goodfellas*, which received six Academy Award nominations, Eppolito played "mobsters, hoodlums and drug dealers," the roles he filled in real life.[58]

Based on the testimony of Kaplan, the drug dealer, Eppolito and Caracappa, at their 2006 trial, were found guilty and sentenced to life imprisonment. In one of the killings, they used flashing lights from their police car to stop a man and take him to an auto body shop in Brooklyn, where Santoro shot and killed him.[59]

Another of the murders occurred on October 31, 1986, just four days prior to when the marine reported seeing Barry Gibbs drop the body. Santoro, Eppolito, and Caracappa captured the victim and rammed him into the trunk of a car. They delivered him to Kaplan in a Toys R Us parking lot, and Kaplan turned the hapless man over to an underboss of the Lucchese family, Anthony "Gaspipe" Casso (because he used a pipe as a weapon), who tortured and killed the victim.

In 1998, before Kaplan agreed to cooperate with the government, Casso was interviewed for the CBS news program *60 Minutes*. By then, he was serving a life sentence after admitting to thirty-six murders. Apparently hoping for leniency from prosecutors in exchange for future testimony, Casso told his interviewer, Ed Bradley, "I have two detectives that work the major squad team for the New York Police Department…Lou Eppolito and Steve—he's got a long last name, Ca…Capis."

"Caracappa?"

"Caracappa yeah. Caracappa, whatever it is. I can't say it all the time you know. Louis is a big guy who works out. Steve is a little small skinny guy." As far as it went, that was an accurate description of the detectives.

About one deceased victim who was in the trunk of a car, Jimmy Hydell, Casso said, "They put him in the car. The kid thought they were taking him to the station house. But they took him to a garage. When they got to the garage, they laid him on the floor; they tied his feet, his handcuffs, put him in the trunk of the car. After that, I killed the kid. Myself, at that time I gave Louis and Steve, I think, $45,000 for delivering him to me."[60]

From 1986 to 1990, the detectives worked for the Lucchese family, including one mistaken killing on Christmas Day of 1986 of a telephone installer who had the same name, Nicholas Guido, as the rival they intended to kill.[61] Kaplan said this job was one he always regretted. By 1996, both Eppolito and Caracappa had retired from the NYPD and moved to Las Vegas, where they lived in houses across the street from each other and engaged in petty drug dealing, according to federal prosecutors. By 2004, Kaplan was back in prison and suffering from prostate cancer, with over eighteen years remaining on his sentence, when he decided to cooperate with the government and testify against the detectives.

FBI agents contacted the jogging marine, who then said that he had identified Gibbs only after Eppolito threatened him and his family. In 2006, the *New York Times* reported on an unusual courtroom exchange between Gibbs and Eppolito at Eppolito's sentencing hearing: "It was at this point that without warning and certainly without permission, a large man wearing a seashell necklace suddenly stood up."

Gibbs yelled, "Mr. Eppolito! Do you remember me?"

"No," said Eppolito.

"I'm the guy you put away for 19 years! I'm Barry Gibbs! You don't remember me? You don't remember what you did to me? To my family?"

Eppolito said he did not remember Gibbs.[62]

WHO KILLED VIRGINIA ROBERTSON?

Since the release of Barry Gibbs from prison, no one has been arrested for killing the victim, Virginia Robertson. Though the marine recanted his statements and testimony implicating Gibbs, he told police on the day of the killing, before encountering Eppolito, that the man who dropped the body from the car was wearing a plaid shirt and red pants. The Innocence Project, a legal defense program at Cardozo Law School in New York, assisted Gibbs after courts had rejected all his legal appeals. At one time on its website, the Innocence Project questioned the evidence against Gibbs, but its summary seemed to implicate him:

> During the search [of Gibbs's home in 1986], police found a pair of red jeans that matched eyewitness testimony of what the perpetrator was wearing during the crime; however, the jeans did not fit Gibbs. Police also discovered that Gibbs owned a gray car [Oldsmobile Cutlass] like the perpetrator's car but Gibbs' car was inoperable, had two flat tires, and had not been driven for a substantial amount of time.[63]

In 2010, the city and state of New York settled a civil case with Gibbs for $11.8 million.[64] As part of that case and prior to the settlement, I was deposed by one of Gibbs's attorneys, Nick Brustin. Toward the end of the deposition, Brustin diverted from asking me questions about facts and asked for my opinion.

> Q. And you would agree that assuming Mr. Gibbs was innocent, a man in his situation, unfamiliar with the criminal justice system, would have no idea how you would go about investigating his innocence, correct?
>
> A. At that point, no, incorrect. At that point all the evidence pointed to Mr. Gibbs having killed the woman.
>
> Q. Do you believe as you sit here today that he committed this crime?
>
> A. But are you asking me whether there's a basis for a determination that he's factually innocent?
>
> Q. Yes.

> A. I don't think there's a basis for that.... I'm more than willing to keep an open mind, and one must keep an open mind. I don't have all the evidence in front of me.

Mr. Gibbs was then sitting at the far, opposite end of a long table from me and next to another of his attorneys, Jennifer Laurin, who is now a law professor at the University of Texas. Gibbs started fidgeting in his chair. He was half-standing when he interrupted and began to yell at me. The court reporter transcribed the interaction:

> Barry Gibbs: Would you like it if it happened to your father?
>
> Mr. Brustin: Stop. Stop. You can't do it here.
>
> Barry Gibbs: Come on. Will you, please. I got to walk out before I get crazy. It should happen to your son, that's what it should happen to, or your family.

Gibbs then walked out of the conference room.

"Stop. Stop. You can't do it here," Brustin told Gibbs.

Maybe Brustin had experienced *it* previously or was referring to Gibbs's interruption at Eppolito's sentencing hearing. Like the character who elicited the response, "The Lady doth protest too much, methinks," in Shakespeare's *Hamlet,* was Barry Gibbs's outburst in the courtroom and interruption during the deposition a performance for the benefit of the public and his attorneys because he surmised that's how an innocent person would act?

In 2025, a former *New York Times* editor, Michael Cannell, published a book, *Blood and the Badge: The Mafia, Two Killer Cops, and a Scandal That Shocked the Nation,* in which he chronicled the exploits of detectives Eppolito and Caracappa. In his investigation, Cannell discovered additional information.

Gibbs, with one son, was a divorced, thirty-eight-year-old navy veteran, addicted to crack at the time that Virginia Robertson was killed on November 4, 1986. Gibbs had worked as a mailman, got suspended, and then worked at a deli. Prior to Virginia Robertson's death, Gibbs had been with a woman for eight years, but they split up after he pushed through her apartment door, which hit her in the nose and broke it. (Detective Stephen Caracappa took the woman's statement at the hospital.)

In April 1986, the woman drove to Gibbs's apartment building and walked to his door and knocked. Gibbs opened the door and was naked. The woman saw another woman with no front teeth inside who looked as though she was high. There was a crack pipe on a desk.

The woman who was killed six months later, Robertson, was a woman with no front teeth. One reason why police suspected Gibbs initially was that prostitutes had told them that a man resembling Barry Gibbs liked rough sex acts.

Cannell's book implies that Detective Eppolito framed Barry Gibbs to protect a Mafia associate who killed Virginia Robertson, which was the claim of Gibbs's lawyers in the civil case. Though there was little or no evidence of that, even if everyone believed Eppolito coerced the marine to identify Gibbs at the precinct, all the other evidence pointed only to Gibbs as the killer and no one else, including his video statement about smoking crack with the victim. The jailhouse informant (though informants must be thoroughly examined) testified that Gibbs admitted to the killing.

Regardless of whether the conviction of Barry Gibbs was correct, the case illustrates the high costs to society when relying on people like Eppolito, who are low in humility, empathy, fairness, and trust (HEFT), the attributes of success in the Decision-Making Formula. Eppolito's bad behavior led either to convicting an innocent man in the first instance or exonerating a guilty man in the second.

The story shows why you should be exceedingly careful in selecting the people who will accompany you through life. Frank Santoro was the prison pal of Burton Kaplan, the drug dealer. One day in early 2001, a Mafia killer riddled Santoro with three shotgun slugs while Santoro walked his dog in the Bronx. The motive for the killing was that another mobster believed Santoro was planning to kidnap his son. Santoro's wife heard the shotgun blasts, rushed outside, and found Santoro dead at age forty-five. Police detectives considered it a "low-level" Mafia rubout.[65] That's not much of a legacy for Santoro.

Burton Kaplan, who turned informant and testified against detectives Eppolito and Caracappa, lived at an undisclosed location for the final three years of his life. A judge had reduced his sentence from twenty-seven to nine years as a reward for testifying against the detectives. Kaplan died from prostate cancer in 2009, at age seventy-five.

Eppolito's partner, Caracappa, died from cancer in a prison hospital on April 8, 2017, at age seventy-five.

Barry Gibbs, who suffered from colon cancer, died a free man in Florida on March 23, 2018, at age sixty-nine.

Detective Eppolito died from heart disease in prison on November 3, 2019, at age seventy-one.

The last to die was Gaspipe Casso, who had killed thirty-six people. After serving twenty-six years of a life sentence, Casso, with prostate cancer and bladder disease, died in prison from COVID-19 in 2020, at age seventy-five.

Although the experiences of most people are less colorful, each of us should ask where we would be now if we had made a different decision about an important matter, such as a job or a relationship. Assume you have one ability that places you in the top 50 percent of everyone with a job similar to yours, and you have experience that will allow you to advance. Equally beneficial, unlike Detective Eppolito, you embody humility, empathy, fairness, and trust.

If, nonetheless, you're not satisfied or not happy, consider whether you are being held back by one of the seven fundamentals of failure (silence, human error, incompetence, isolation, inaction, fear, or falsity). You might have found it difficult previously to identify why you're not happy, but in applying the formula you'll find a way to express what's holding you back, as well as a new course that could lead to better results. During the journey, try to stay away from people who might try to hurt you.

Key Points

- In evaluating or judging people, their mental states are usually more revealing than their actions.
- Respond when someone tries intentionally to hurt you.
- Do not allow unreasonable fear to prevent you from responding.
- If a response cannot improve your conditions, your choices are to stay and remain silent or leave the environment.
- Every act has costs and benefits: weigh them carefully, but don't procrastinate.

CHAPTER 3

DON'T SAY SORRY WHEN MY LIFE DEPENDS ON YOU

(PLANNING FOR EMERGENCIES)

Unlike the men from Brooklyn, most people will try to save each other if they can do so without risking harm to themselves or others close to them. A few will sacrifice their lives for strangers. But how should people, if they have discretion or authority, decide whether someone should be saved or allowed to die, or possibly hurt or killed to protect others, such as in self-defense? In the previous chapter, Detective Eppolito and the others, as their carnage cascaded over the years, deceived everyone around them. In the case ahead, government doctors had to decide whether to save someone they believed should be allowed to die, as unusual as that seems. In deciding whether to act against their belief, a crisis put them in a position to consciously select one of the fundamentals of failure, falsity.

After Osama bin Laden organized the airplane attacks on the World Trade Center and the Pentagon on September 11, 2001, the US military, in October, attacked the Taliban rulers in Afghanistan. American troops quickly dispatched the Taliban government and pursued bin Laden, who made a narrow escape through the mountains. American military forces found and killed bin Laden in Pakistan in 2011. Before the military withdrew from Afghanistan in August 2021, America tried to install a democratic government and establish a stable economy. The endeavor, Operation Enduring Freedom, was unsuccessful, and during the mission, over 2,400 US soldiers were killed, as well as a larger number of civilian military contractors.

As part of Enduring Freedom, some faculty members from West Point volunteered to help establish a new military academy in Kabul. The program originated with the dean of academics, Brigadier General Dan Kaufman, and continued with the next dean, Brigadier General Pat Finnegan, who approved my participation. In 2007, I traveled to Kabul and created the department of law at the Afghan academy.

After training sessions taught by cadets who were on the rifle team, I qualified at the shooting range to carry a handgun, a requirement of Department of Defense personnel who accompanied US soldiers. With army reservists and National Guard soldiers, and a fellow civilian professor, Stanley (pseudonym), I attended one week of training at Fort Benning, in Georgia, though there wasn't time to receive instruction on how to identify roadside bombs. We flew from Atlanta to Baltimore and eventually boarded the Patriot Express, a large jet operated by a government contractor, and then flew with a couple hundred soldiers to Germany, Turkey, and Kyrgyzstan, where we waited a few days for a C-5 military transport plane to take soldiers to Bagram Air Base, which was just over an hour's drive north of Kabul. At Bagram, we waited a couple of days for a convoy, which consisted of three small Toyota SUVs and a few soldiers with long guns, to drive to Kabul on a highway often littered with roadside bombs.

We made our way to Camp Eggers, the main US base in Kabul, where I was Stanley's roommate inside a cargo container outside Eggers. Military contractors convert metal containers, like those on ocean-going ships and freight trains, into living quarters, with two single beds, two storage racks, a divider between the beds, and sometimes a window with an air conditioner. The dining facility and all other utilities and stores were inside Eggers, which meant that two or three times each day we'd move between the containers and Eggers.

The short trip was not relaxing. Afghan security personnel guarded the containers, interspersed over several blocks, and we had to dash across a long, open street before ducking behind the barriers of Eggers. On the days we traveled to the grounds of the National Military Academy, about a half-hour drive away, we had to leave from and return to Eggers. Getting stuck in traffic or moving slowly were undesirable events.

The Afghans who guarded the US personnel staying in the cargo containers outside Camp Eggers were influenced by Taliban rule, which began in the early 1990s and ended in 2001, before resuming in 2021. As part of their interpretation of the Koran, the Taliban prohibit not only photographs but also mirrors, despite their invention about eight thousand years ago in Turkey.[66] The Taliban reason that representation of a live human, especially women, can lead to vice and a lack of virtue. As a result, some Afghans have not viewed their own faces.[67]

Stanley, my roommate, was a great guy, but at night, instead of walking down the steps and to another cargo container next door that had toilets and a shower, he'd urinate in a bottle that he kept alongside his loaded nine-millimeter pistol. I hoped not to awaken him at night, and I avoided our cargo container as much as possible and, when not at the military academy, spent most of my free time inside Eggers. I'd exercise in the gym and then walk to a cargo container inside the base to take a shower, usually from between 10:00 p.m. and midnight. In my sweaty shorts and shirt in the cold air, I'd have to cart my gear—body armor, helmet, pistol, two magazines with cartridges, baggy military shirt, and pants—because once I left Eggers, I'd need to cross the no-man's-land of a road alone at about midnight before I'd find the Afghan guards who surrounded the cargo containers.

One night, at about 11:00 p.m., after working out in the gym, I carried my gear like firewood and walked up the steps of the cargo container to the showers. On previous nights, I had not encountered anyone else, but this time I heard shuffling from inside. I placed my gear on the top few steps of the stairway, gripped the pistol, and opened the unlocked door about two inches. When I looked inside the lighted shower room, my concern was alleviated. I grabbed my gear and trudged into the container to meet the US military officer that I had identified by the rank insignia on the shoulder of a shirt laid over a bench that held his clothes.

Tired but now wide awake late at night, I would soon hear a disturbing story about the treatment of a person. Perhaps equally troubling is that few people will agree on whether he had been mistreated. The officer was slightly surprised but then relieved when he heard me speak. We exchanged the usual pleasantries, our home states, jobs, and what we were doing in Afghanistan. He was a military officer-doctor practicing in a medical specialty that is in great demand during a war. As a result, US doctors in the specialties could negotiate with the military to serve short stints, such as this officer's six months, and then return to their medical practices in the US.

He said that he was down in Kabul for the day but worked regularly at the hospital at Bagram Air Base. The doctors and nurses at Bagram were proud that their professional ethics required them to treat anyone who came through the doors, Americans and Afghans, as well as enemy Taliban fighters. I think that's probably true, but, as you will see, some patients, perhaps understandably when rules don't tell us what to do, were treated differently depending on whose side they were on.[68]

The officer continued dressing but did not rush to finish our conversation. I arranged my gear and clothes around a couple of hooks so that I'd be in position to dress and leave soon after showering. He dallied and seemed to want to talk.

Curious, I asked, "What's the strangest thing you've seen in Afghanistan? Doctors like you must be in the middle of everything bad here."

He nodded, and his face showed concern, like a weather reporter explaining the likely path of a hurricane. He seemed not to want to be connected to the story that he was about to tell, but he wanted someone to know it for fear it would not be revealed.

"I was in the hospital," he said, "working on a surgical team. The military police brought us a Taliban boy bombmaker, a teenager, no older than that, who had been making bombs in a hut."

"Dangerous job."

"One of the bombs exploded on the boy, blowing off all his arms and legs. The MPs brought us only his head and torso, connected. Alive."

"If you survive, that will be a hard life."

"That's what we thought."

This man, probably in his thirties, looked down. I think he was asking himself whether he was a military officer or a doctor first. The ethics of the professions are different. Soldiers are permitted to kill people intentionally. Doctors try to save everyone.

But there is one exception for doctors and, thus, one similarity. Both soldiers and doctors, though for different reasons, as you will see, sometimes do nothing and knowingly allow people to die.

The doctor wanted to talk more, but he needed the smallest acknowledgment. I asked the obvious question because it seemed he wouldn't speak without it. "What did you do with him?"

The doctor was glad to tell me. "From the MPs, we knew the boy was from Pakistan and learning from a Taliban operator how to construct roadside bombs to use against us. He was nearly dead when we got him. Unconscious, he couldn't tell us what he wanted. No parents. We got together a medical ethics team fast to decide what to do. If we treated and saved him, the Afghans have no social services and would leave him on the border with Pakistan. He'd die from exposure and no care. Who can get food with no arms and no legs?"

"Hungry, and you can't move."

Recalling US constitutional law, a course that I taught, I said, "A doctor's patient has a right to refuse treatment if that's what he wants."

Doctors usually have a very good grasp of the law that affects their practices, and the right-to-die principle is well known. But this case presented an additional factor.

The officer-doctor was silent, so I filled the void. "But this guy can't tell you what he wants, and there's nobody to speak for him."

"Correct."

"You, the doctors, had to decide."

"We had to decide what was in his best interest," said the doctor. "What would he want? To live or die?" (A legal rule, *parens patriae*, authorizes societal authorities, like physicians, usually with a judge's order, to act on behalf of children and incapacitated adults if there is no one to decide on their behalf.)

"I think most people would say, 'Let me go,'" I said.

The doctor nodded silently but waited to speak. I wondered why he would make me ask the next, obvious question again when he realized that anyone would want to know what had happened to the boy. But people think and act at different speeds, though you will see in a moment that, to make a correct decision, they should have some prior preparation.

"What did you decide to do with him?"

Partly relieved, he said, "The ethical team's decision was to withhold medical treatment."

"That's reasonable."

The doctor was silent again. Midnight was the top of the next hour, and only a few insomniacs in the recreation center and soldiers guarding the perimeter of Camp Eggers were awake. But he looked over his shoulder, toward the showers, and swiveled to look at the door opposite, as though the Taliban were at the precipice.

There had to be something else on his mind.

The doctor's telling of the story, interspersed with his hesitation, might allow us to infer a more disturbing ending. This provides a moment to evaluate how the seven fundamentals of failure can affect someone's life. Though you do not yet have all the facts, try to predict generally what issues might arise.

The doctors at the Bagram base were confronted with a vexing ethical issue: whether to withhold treatment from a patient they could save. In a war zone and with no time to spare, they formed an ethics committee and decided not to save the Taliban teenager, a decision that was consistent with their personal and professional values. The doctors collaborated, spoke freely, and acted according to their collective conscience. Two of the positive variables were obviously present: high-ability physicians who possessed the attributes of success, especially empathy toward the boy, but also humility, fairness, and trust. Regarding the third variable (observations/practices), while the doctors were experienced in practicing medicine, they had not encountered a case like this one.

Nonetheless, everyone in a job will sooner or later see something new; the doctors had about as much experience as anyone could. These conditions promote correct decision-making, especially because the fundamentals of failure do not seem to be present, at least not the first six of them (silence, human error, incompetence, isolation, inaction, and fear).

> This leaves us to consider the seventh fundamental of failure, falsity. Part of falsity consists of knowingly accepting an undesirable circumstance, outcome, or relationship. If you're feeling great about almost everything but still have some anxiety, a good question to ask is whether I'm being true to myself.

With the military doctors, if you've eliminated all the fundamentals of failure except falsity, then, given this doctor's trepidation in the cargo container, something from the outside might have introduced falsity into the decision-making process at the hospital in Bagram. Working for the US military, the doctors were subject to pressure not felt by doctors who work in civilian hospitals. In the military, doctors and everyone else are constantly subjected to powerful peer pressure, informal customs, and formal orders of everyone higher in rank. It becomes easier to see how such circumstances can lead some people, probably most, to act against their consciences when they are pressured by peers or superiors.

This reasoning brings us closer to a prediction about what happened and helps you understand how you can be influenced by others. One of the most difficult obstacles in understanding why we act against our conscience is our unwillingness to admit how much control other people have over us. But most of the time, that's only because we've relinquished to them a portion of our being. This officer's angst inside the cargo container seemed to indicate an outside influence that had affected his judgment, as well as a result that he had come to regret.

"There's more to the story?" I asked him.

The doctor nodded and buttoned his shirt.

"After we met and made our decision," he said, "we were waiting around the hospital for the kid to die and the next patient to come in. But then officers from Military Intelligence came to the hospital because they had found out about the boy."

Now more a doctor than an officer, he tried to be clinical, as though explaining to medical students a course of treatment for a patient. Speaking was a method to expel from his brain what he wanted to forget but couldn't.

"MI said they wanted us to save the boy so they could interrogate him about bombmakers in Afghanistan."

"You had decided not to treat the boy because that's what he'd want if he could speak."

"The MI officers told us that by saving the boy for their interrogation of him, we might save US soldiers from roadside bombs."

The doctor lapsed into another moment of silence. He didn't want to speak much longer. Again, he made me ask the obvious question.

"What happened?"

He finished dressing and was stretching an arm into a jacket. "We saved the boy so that he could be interrogated."

"That's an interesting story," I said.

"Nice to meet you," he answered.

"Same here."

He walked out of the cargo container, and I took a shower.

Many people preach to do the right thing. But that mantra is near meaningless because most decisions are easy, such as whether or not to steal or harm another person. The remaining problems are more complicated and often have many plausible solutions. They require significant analysis and the perspectives of informed people before a correct decision can be obtained. Moreover, we cannot usually find the best answer through resorting to intuition, which is simply a conclusion or decision based on relatively few facts.

If the military doctors at the hospital in Bagram in 2007 believed they were doctors first, we could ask one question. How could doctors justify saving the life of a boy if they believed he would, if conscious, decline treatment to avoid suffering alone later in the wilds in the hours prior to his death on the border with Pakistan?

If they believed they were military officers first, we could ask a different question. How could a military officer justify *not* saving the boy for interrogation to help save the lives of fellow American soldiers?

In the end, these decision-makers seemed to tell us they were officers before doctors. In saving the teenager for interrogation, they acted against their medical ethics decision.

There was more evidence of this during the same war in Afghanistan, just over four years later, in 2011. The US military then broadcast that it had a policy to treat wounded and captured enemy combatants the same way it treats American soldiers. But you've just observed that similar treatment was not provided in one instance at Bagram in 2007. But in 2011, the American Forces Press Service, part of the US Department of Defense, filed an article titled "Bagram Hospital Provides Care to All Who Need It," on the medical treatment of detainees or enemy combatants in Afghanistan.

The hospital's commander, Lieutenant Colonel (Dr.) Guillermo Tellez, walked through the hospital with a reporter. They observed an enemy detainee "hooked up to all kinds of medical equipment—breathing tubes, intravenous feeding tubes, the works"—and guarded by a military police soldier, according to the reporter.

Paraphrasing LTC Tellez, the reporter wrote that the "patient was a detainee" who "was picked up during an operation and brought to the hospital to receive the same level of care provided to every wounded U.S. and coalition service member and every Afghan security force member or civilian brought to the facility."

The reporter again paraphrased LTC/Dr. Tellez. "No other country in the world adheres so closely to that ethical standard, Colonel Tellez said."

It "can be hard" to care for a detainee, according to Colonel Tellez. "We know he may have been involved in hurting our own. Only in America. It is truly what makes us special. We care for all."[69]

That aspiration, caring for all, comes with exceptions. Regarding the teenager with no arms and legs, the US military doctors at Bagram, where Colonel Tellez worked later, cared for the boy differently because he was not a wounded US soldier or a soldier in an allied force. In treating him differently, the doctors at Bagram might have violated the rule that military personnel must act according to the laws of armed conflict (based on treaties among nations and customs developed during wars), a body of law that is also referred to as international humanitarian law (IHL). Under these rules, enemy soldiers "who cannot fight due to being sick, wounded, captured or incapacitated...are not allowed to be attacked or harmed because they pose no threat. The rules of IHL state that these individuals are to be treated humanely and protected from harm."[70]

We are left with the ironic question of whether the doctors' treatment of the Taliban teenager and saving his life, which is almost always their primary goal, was ultimately harmful to him. Was their treatment of him a violation of the laws of armed conflict because they treated a "sick, wounded, captured or incapacitated" enemy soldier differently than they would have treated a US soldier? The primary point to consider here is the cost of acting against your conscience, against what you believe to be right. How well can you justify, rectify, or forget an act that, when you did it, you believed to be wrong?

A MORPHINE ALTERNATIVE?

Many years earlier, through handling homicide cases in Brooklyn, my eyes had been opened wider to decision-making surrounding death. Later, after I began teaching, a civic organization once invited me to speak at its luncheon about ethical dilemmas in dying. Several nurses were seated with me at a large round table prior to my presentation and spoke matter-of-factly about the use of morphine in the treatment of dying patients.

About half of the US states have laws or are considering laws concerning medically assisted death. Often near the end of life and isolated in nursing homes, hospitals, and other settings, terminally ill people will come to wish they could die sooner than when nature would run its course. What should then happen when a person and her family members (altruistically) prefer an early death? The legal answer is nothing because helping someone die sooner than what is natural will expose the helper, no matter how compassionate, to a homicide charge.[71]

Hospice providers, in assuaging the grief of family members, want to assure everyone that morphine, a powerful but common painkiller for dying patients, will not hasten death. The following explanation by a hospice provider describes the use of morphine when someone you love is close to death. What two words in the explanation below reveal how some medical professionals might use morphine outside the law but within the confines of what many, perhaps most, people would consider to be right?

> There is no evidence that opioids such as morphine hasten the dying process when a person receives the right dose to control the symptoms he or she is experiencing. In fact, research suggests that using opioids to treat pain or shortness of breath near the end of life may help a person live a bit longer. Pain and shortness of breath are exhausting, and people nearing the end of life have limited strength and energy. So, it makes sense that treating these symptoms might slow down the rate of decline, if only for a few hours.[72]

The "right dose" of morphine, as noted in the first sentence, will not hasten death. However, a higher, not right, dose of morphine may, indeed, lead to an early death.

A jury in Ohio, in 2022, found a physician, Dr. William Hussel, not guilty of fourteen counts of murder after the prosecution accused him of overdosing to death with fentanyl and other pain-relieving drugs fourteen critically ill patients. The prosecution's argument was that, unless a state authorizes early death, the administration of a drug that hastens death is an intentional killing, murder, including when the terminally ill person wants to die immediately.[73]

You should expect that someday a medical professional will ask you about the use of morphine. To help process that question before then, perhaps you could apply the Decision-Making Formula to that issue or other issues that you foresee might be on your horizon. Simply start by assessing your abilities and go from there.

> If (natural abilities + attributes of success) + (observations/practices) > (fundamentals of failure) = correct decision-making.

Regarding the military doctors in Afghanistan, the only fundamental of failure that seemed to be present among them is falsity, in that the doctors' actions in saving the teenager were contrary to what they believed. The Decision-Making Formula permits you to arrive at what you believe is the best possible decision given any problem. But it cannot measure for you the mental and emotional costs of not acting according to your conscience. We know from the doctors in Afghanistan and their patient, the teenager, that the costs can be very high.

Key Points

- You will face an emergency that requires a decision.
- Adopt a decision-making formula now.
- Know how to respond when someone, such as an employer, urges or expects you to act against your conscience.
- Decide how, if necessary, you will care for someone close to you.
- Communicate your wishes now in anticipation that someone will need to care for you in the future.

CHAPTER 4

THE SILENCE OF FEAR

(FINDING YOUR CONSCIENCE)

In this chapter, we see how people use fear to induce others to remain silent. This leads to more fear because people who believe they are alone in their thoughts are less likely to take any kind of action that would increase their courage and security. Throughout history, speaking and other forms of expression, followed by contrary opinions, have been the best ways to improve individually and advance civilization, as well as to prevent others from hurting us. That's because speaking and sharing experiences and knowledge allow us to form alliances.

In contrast, censors or controllers, who are often partners and supervisors, as well as government officials, try to exercise control over other people to alleviate their own insecurity, protect their own interests, and signal that they have more power than others in their group. Thus, the consideration of fear in this chapter will allow you to see how just one of the fundamentals of failure alone can be disabling and lead to a second failure, silence. When people experience fear and silence simultaneously, then almost all of them will be disabled emotionally and unable to fully access their abilities and attributes. Correct decision-making then becomes difficult, and often impossible.

We should be especially vigilant when people try to instill fear by invoking one of the five primal apprehensions that populate nightmares: fear of dying, mutilation, abandonment, rejection, and humiliation.[74] Unlike in the past, your competitors, given today's legal protections, might not have the right or ability to take your property by force. But with similar dire consequences, they, especially employers, may terminate you at any moment and threaten your livelihood, creating possibly the most stinging fear in modern life.

Trying to escape the Great Depression and alleviate the hardships of older people, Congress and President Franklin D. Roosevelt, in 1935, created the Social Security system. In a 1937 case that upheld the Social Security Act as a constitutional method of taxation, Justice Benjamin Cardozo, writing for the Supreme Court, explained how money can alleviate fear: "The hope behind this statute is to save men and women from the rigors of the poor house, as well as from the haunting fear that such a lot awaits them when journey's end is near."[75]

The risk of job loss is much greater in the US than in other Western countries because most jobs in America are considered to be at-will, which means that a private employer may legally terminate an employee for almost any reason.[76] Many workers who perform ably and are compliant with the formal and informal rules of an organization may retain their jobs—but only if they do not dissent or complain and relinquish what is perhaps their most valuable intangible possession: speaking freely according to their conscience.

Given the idiosyncratic skills needed in an industrial society, along with our inability to live off the land if our employment is terminated, almost all people will accept the mental and emotional headache, which does not subside, that accompanies silence so as not to offend an employer or someone who can influence their economic well-being. In this way, the greatest imminent threat to every person remains the same as it has been throughout history: other people. Five scholars described the practical, external source of fear:

- "Fear…evolved to protect animals against environmental threats."
- "The function most frequently associated with fear is protection from threat."
- "Fear…is a conscious awareness that you are in harm's way."
- "'Fear' is the combination of defensive responses—physiological, behavioral and…the conscious experience and interpretations of these responses—that are stimulated by specific stimuli."
- "Fear is an intensely negative internal state. It…arouse[s] our peak performance for avoidance, escape or confrontation."[77]

Our acknowledgment of fear and economic vulnerability is humbling because it exposes how much control other people have over us in the workplace and within close relationships.

Sometimes you can overcome fear. One of the scientists who conducted a 2025 study on innate fear said, "We've uncovered the mechanism by which the brain—through experience—can understand which potential instinctive dangers are actually not a danger." The scientists found that they could train mice, which are afraid of shadows, to continue their normal foraging activities even when a shadow is approaching them, implying that people can be trained to ignore their unreasonable perceptions of a threat.[78]

Probably the most effective way to overcome fear is through communication. In a marriage, according to a 2007 study, "women who 'self-silenced' during conflict with their spouse, compared with women who did not, had four times the risk of dying. Men with wives who were upset by work were 2.7 times more likely to develop CHD [coronary heart disease]."[79]

Though Americans crow about freedom of expression, established in the First Amendment in 1791, they would be surprised that the US is ranked number fifty-seven in press freedom among 180 countries, according to the 2024 report of Reporters Without Borders. The US is second to last, ahead of only Greece at number eighty-nine, among all Western countries.[80]

Friedrich-Alexander-Universität, in Germany, compiles the Academic Freedom Index, which measures "freedom to research and teach; freedom of academic exchange and dissemination; institutional autonomy; campus integrity; and freedom of academic and cultural expression."[81] Among 179 countries ranked in the index in 2025, the US was number eighty-five and, again, second to last among all Western countries (behind only Greece, at number ninety-two).[82]

The trend toward less freedom of expression in the US is increasing, and this was before the Trump administration assumed office in January 2025. In a poll from 1954, at the height of McCarthyism, 13 percent of the American respondents indicated less willingness to speak up when answering the following question:

> What about you personally? Do you or don't you feel as free to speak your mind as you used to?[83]

Answering the same question in a 2020 poll, 46 percent of the American respondents indicated they felt less free to speak, a 254 percent increase in people who feel less free.

According to the researchers for their 2022 study on the matter, "Keeping Your Mouth Shut: Spiraling Self-Censorship in the United States," the "findings suggest that one's larger macro-environment may have little to do with self-censorship. Instead, micro-environment sentiments, such as worrying that expressing unpopular views will isolate and alienate people from their friends, family, and neighbors, may be the driver of self-censorship."[84]

In measuring how much expressive freedom you possess, consider how you compare to the people inside the most censorious institution, the US military. In twenty-six years at West Point, I've worked closely with hundreds of army officers and observed thousands of others in small and large meetings, including officers who were commissioned as long ago as the Vietnam War era, which began in the 1960s. I have not heard one officer ever say to any higher-ranking officer, including on the most minor matter, even regarding which sports team is best, "I disagree," or any similar expression.

One method used broadly in American society today to exert control over other people is to characterize their expression as behavior and claim that it, behavior (which is really words or writings), is dangerous or hurtful and should be banned or the speaker punished. This allegation has been employed by students at colleges, including by cadets at West Point. Unlike the military instructors, who are subject to the military's penal code and can be criminally prosecuted for uttering truthful speech that the superintendent considers to be disrespectful, the civilian instructors there are not subject to the penal code. It would seem that they would be more likely to speak up and be able to resist censorship. But, in fact, and this is a lesson to everyone in a structured environment, they remain as silent as the military officers.

One method employed by the senior military administrators at West Point is to institute formal investigations to determine whether to punish civilian instructors for any number of alleged infractions, including speaking inappropriately or without the approval of the administrators. The primary method is called a 15-6 investigation (fifteen-dash-six in army parlance). Elsewhere in the army, this type of investigation is used to collect evidence surrounding the most serious matters, including homicides. One 15-6 investigation, for example, concerned soldiers in an army gunship who, during the war in Afghanistan in 2015, fired cannons for thirty minutes (according to the army) or sixty minutes (according to Doctors Without Borders) on a hospital in Kunduz, Afghanistan, and mistakenly killed forty-two doctors, nurses, and patients. Based on the 15-6 report about the killings, the army did not charge any soldier or officer with a crime.[85]

For civilian instructors, who, unlike military instructors, are not entitled to free government-funded legal representation, these investigations are intimidating, expensive, and often career-ending. In a one-year period in 2023 and 2024, West Point used 15-6 investigations against at least three instructors, all of whom resigned. All of them were in their sixties, the oldest sixty-nine, and had worked as instructors or for the government for twenty-eight, twenty-nine, and forty-one years. In all instances, the senior military administrators instituted the investigations after military students, the cadets, had objected to something the instructors said.

Another civilian professor, a twenty-year teaching veteran, survived an investigation after several cadets complained that the professor was too demanding and fostered a "toxic environment," a popular expression. After an investigation, the professor received what West Point considers a minimal punishment, a counseling letter in the "local file" (the academic department), which will be destroyed after one year. In essence, the letter is a way for a senior military officer to save face and simultaneously coerce professors to remain silent for at least a year and probably the remainder of their careers, given the residual fear produced by an investigation.

The letter issued to this professor, by a department head, an army colonel, directed the professor to use a better "selection of words" and "tone of voice," an edict seemingly reminiscent of reeducation programs. The colonel further directed the professor not to use "inappropriate phrases."

DEMORALIZATION, RESIGNATION, AND SUICIDE

No matter where or for whom you work or the people and organizations with which you are involved, the investigations and subsequent resignations of the professors show why you cannot be complacent despite, like them, possessing exceptional ability, the attributes of success, and significant experience (observations), which are the positive variables in the Decision-Making Formula.

> If (natural abilities + attributes of success) + (observations/practices) > (fundamentals of failure) = correct decision-making.

The three professors, as well as the fourth one who did not resign, possessed all of those positive variables, but their careers were harmed by two of the fundamentals of failure, silence and fear. The silence and fear were brought to the professors by other people, in fact by senior military officers they believed were their friends. If the professors' words had not been objectionable to someone, if, in essence, they had remained silent, they would not have been investigated. But, after the professors said something that someone did not want to hear, the intimidating investigations induced in them extraordinary fear and anxiety. Just like the psychological response present in our ancestors, fight or flight, the college professors, few of whom are inclined to fight or have adequate resources, believed their only alternative was to flee, to resign, which is what they did.

In any environment in which the people with formal authority are rarely challenged, their aggressive and unchecked behavior will cascade and lead to increasingly severe punishments for other people. Once, at West Point, while teaching a class in a room with large windows for a wall, I glimpsed two men in sport coats standing in the hallway. After the cadets left the classroom, the men walked in and asked to speak with me. Smiling and friendly in the phony way of people who want something for nothing, one said he was an FBI agent, and the other said he worked for the US Army's Criminal Investigation Division. These G-men were conducting a criminal investigation of a civilian professor from whom West Point demanded reimbursement in a pay dispute.

The fear of criminal prosecution inside the military, because the threat is ever-present, is like worrying about being imprisoned if caught pocketing a penny that you found in a parking lot. Though the military rewards soldiers with patches and ribbons for their uniforms, it promotes a punitive culture that relies on negative reinforcement to influence behavior and suppress emotions, feelings, and expression. Soldiers work as hard or harder to avoid punishment and obtain accolades from their superiors as they do to achieve high performance.

The negative reinforcements employed in the military have seeped deep inside American society. For instance, only about 6 percent of the population has served in the military, but about 19 percent of police officers are military veterans. One police psychologist, Matthew Guller, worked with 470 law enforcement agencies. In one period, from 2014 to 2016, in a screening by his firm of about four thousand police applicants, 8.5 percent of military applicants failed a screening, while 4.8 percent of non-veterans failed the screening.[86]

In a 2018 study by the University of Texas, researchers found that military veterans who became police officers were far more likely to fire their guns in the line of duty than officers who were not veterans. The police officers who had not been deployed while in the military were 1.94 times more likely (than non-veterans) to have fired their guns in the line of duty. Officers who had been deployed were 2.9 times more likely to have fired their guns.[87]

Military service members and veterans are far more likely to die by suicide than people who have not served in the military. The spouses and children of active-duty service members are also more likely to die by suicide than a similar cohort in the non-military population. In 2023, the suicide rate for active-duty service members was 28.2 per 100,000 people. (The number of suicide deaths in the military was 513, according to the Department of Defense.)[88]

For 2023, the overall suicide rate in the US was 14.7 per 100,000 people, only 52 percent of the military rate. (The number of suicide deaths in the US in 2023 was 49,316, according to the Centers for Disease Control.)[89]

The suicide rate for military reserve and National Guard personnel, who hold civilian jobs and train only periodically, was 20.9 and 21.2 per 100,000, respectively, also much higher than the rate for people not in the military.[90]

Similarly troubling, the suicide rate for spouses and children of military personnel increased between 2011 and 2022 (5.8 percent in 2022, the most recent reporting year), and such "military dependents overall had a higher suicide rate than comparable U.S. population groups in 2013, 2015, 2018, 2019, and 2020," while "the rate was similar in remaining years," according to the Department of Defense.[91]

The Pentagon believed that "intimate relationship problems" contributed to 44 percent of the suicides of active-duty service members. But today, military families almost always accompany their service members throughout the world, and 92 percent of the suicides of the active-duty personnel occurred in the continental United States.[92] Thus, it's not distance or separation that leads to suicide in the military. The high suicide rates among soldiers and their family members seem more likely to be attributable to dysfunctional interpersonal interactions among members of the military.

The conditions inside the US military, specifically a controlling ethos, in essence a lot of bad leaders, not enemy forces, are the primary reasons why service members kill themselves. A 2023 study in *Psychiatry Research*, comparing active-duty soldiers with civilians, found that neither war nor post-traumatic stress syndrome is the reason for the higher military suicide rate. The study represented "the most extensive historical examination to compare suicide among male active-duty personnel in the U.S. Army to U.S. civilians" from 1900 to 2020. The study concluded that military service members and civilians experience the same social stimuli, but that, nonetheless, military personnel exhibit higher rates of suicide, consistently over a period of 120 years:

> In other words, societal and cultural factors likely play a much larger role in military suicides than the military-specific factors of combat trauma or post-traumatic stress disorder (PTSD) per se.... Rather than understanding military suicides as being primarily driven by combat trauma or PTSD, to be effective, prevention efforts should strive to understand

> military suicides through the lens of larger societal factors.[93]

The study showed that the suicide rates of military personnel and civilians move in tandem, with no spikes attributable to war or PTSD. This indicates that a condition inside the US military that is not present outside the military causes soldiers to kill themselves.

Another 2023 study, published by the *Journal of the American Medical Association*, also showed that war and combat do not affect the suicide rate of military personnel. The researchers found that "of approximately 9.6 million Vietnam War–era veterans, there was no increased risk of suicide mortality among veterans who served in the Vietnam War theater and veterans who served during the Vietnam War but were not deployed to Vietnam."[94]

An additional study, also from 2023, examined the suicide rates of military veterans from 2006 to 2020, during the wars in Afghanistan and Iraq. The study found, "Veterans serving after 9/11 have higher suicide rates compared to the US population."[95]

With combat experience and post-traumatic stress syndrome not the causes of the high suicide rate, the elevated rate must originate in a different stressor inside the military—its controlling ethos, specifically the authoritarian behavior of many military officers and enlisted leaders in all the military branches. Another study from 2023 used data from the US Department of Veterans Affairs and compared the suicide rates of military veterans and civilians from 2017 to 2020. Per 100,000 people, for males aged eighteen to thirty-four, the rate of suicide of military veterans was 51.7, almost double the rate of civilians, at 26.3.

For that period, the military suicide rate, by age, was higher than the civilian rate at all ages, except one. The exception was that after age seventy-five, the civilian suicide rate was higher than the military veterans' rate (46.2 civilian and 33.2 military).[96] It's possible that military veterans are more accepting of their declining physical and mental ability in old age because they learned to accept the loss of autonomy when they were young adults and lived with that deprivation their entire lives.

The problem of suicide, like many others inside the military—sexual assault, hazing, retaliation, and silencing—can be traced to one condition: the desire of soldiers and officers to exercise control over other people. From a soldier's perspective, deliberate cruelty, which is accepted in this environment, is not forgettable. A 2020 study by the National Institute of Justice examined mass public killings of four or more people from 1966 to 2019 and found that one of the most prominent characteristics of the killers was that they had been in the military. Of 172 people who committed public mass shootings, 28.5 percent had a military background, but only about 6 percent of US adults have served in the military.[97]

Soldiers and military veterans are four to five times more likely to be mass killers inside the United States than would be expected given their percentage of the population. They not only kill at disproportionate rates, but they also learn to become among the harshest people in American society. Researchers from a consortium of academic institutions found, "The results of a multivariate analysis reveal that having a U.S. military background is the single strongest individual-level predictor of whether a subject in the PIRUS data [Profiles of Individual Radicalization in the United States] is classified as a mass casualty offender. Of the 451 subjects with military backgrounds...who committed extremist crimes from 1990–2022, 170 (37.7%) are classified as mass casualty offenders. A record of military service is more reliable for classifying mass casualty offenders...than factors that are more commonly discussed in the literature on mass casualty crimes, such as mental health concerns, offending alone or in a small group, and having a pre-radicalization criminal history."[98]

The most salient point is that mistreatment of people in the military is exceedingly destructive for American society. At West Point, the FBI agent's first question to me, whether I knew the professor being investigated, was a ruse because the agents knew that the professor and I had emailed each other over the years we worked and were on a committee together—ironically, the Academic Freedom Advisory Committee. Government agents often want an interviewee to lie because they can then threaten to prosecute the interviewee for lying to an agent unless he informs on their target.

The agents knew the location of my classroom and when the class would end, and they were operating inside my department's physical space. This information and permission could have come only from the head of my department, an army colonel. They knew my whereabouts the previous year when I had been on a sabbatical (when teachers conduct research). If they and the army officers were not trying to hurt me, they would have provided advance notice so we could schedule a meeting at a mutually convenient time.

The FBI agent asked, "Did you visit the professor during your sabbatical?"

The CID agent asked, "Do you send emails to the professor?"

From a stack of papers about two inches thick, which he pushed toward me on the table, he said, "Do you recognize any of these?"

I flipped through a few pages and knew these investigators had obtained all the emails of the professor, including those to and from me, over the years. I pushed back the stack and told the agents that I wouldn't speak to them about the professor.

The FBI agent said, "We could subpoena you to the grand jury if you don't speak."

"That's a great idea," I said. "As a prosecutor, I presented about two hundred cases to grand juries. I'll ask the judge who supervises the grand jury to appoint an attorney for me, and we'll see if you have the authority to compel my testimony."

The FBI agent said, "I don't think we'll have to do that."

The army criminal investigator collected his papers. They stood and started shuffling out of the classroom. Trying to make nice, the FBI agent told me, "If your students had seen this, they would have learned a lot."

In early 2025, West Point's senior military officers responded to what they believed might be necessary to protect their interests, given new scrutiny of the military academies by the Trump administration. An investigative reporter, Jasper Cravens, had been collecting data on education at the academies, and he tried to attend the West Point graduation ceremony on May 24, 2025, when President Trump was the guest speaker. But West Point denied Cravens a press pass. In August 2025, Cravens wrote an article for *Politico*, "Inside Pete Hegseth's Civilian Purge at West Point."

Cravens reported on the activities surrounding Trump's speech, including protestors who gathered outside West Point on graduation day. Cravens wrote, "Within the pack of protesters was a masked figure dressed entirely in black. He was a civilian West Point professor, someone who wanted to protest Trump's speech but was anxious over the campus crackdown, and fearful about retaliation. 'It's dark days in there,' he told me. I understood the worries of the professor in black. They were echoed throughout my interviews for this story. Still, I wondered if maybe his anonymous get-up was a bit of an overreaction."

But anyone who has worked around controlling people or been in a controlling relationship knows the necessity of caution, which

Cravens soon understood. He wrote further, "My mind changed six days later, when it became apparent that I myself had been monitored. That morning, a Secret Service agent showed up to my parents' door, explaining that West Point had reported me for acting suspiciously. Specifically, they alleged that I'd been asking people to speak with the president. This wasn't true, and the service declined to discuss the intelligence undergirding the allegation. But it felt like a poetic charge in light of my reportorial focus on the military's stifling of academic inquiry. Certainly, any reporter, as with any pupil, must be allowed, encouraged even, to ask probing questions."[99]

THE MARCH OF VIOLENCE

After 15-6 and criminal investigations, the blunter instrument used by people in the military is violence, against their colleagues. Once, on entering the main gate at West Point in December 2018, a military police soldier told me that he had selected my car for a search and that I'd be delayed. I asked him what method he used to select cars to search, such as license plate numbers that end with odd or even numbers or every fifth car, for example, to ensure that the police do not single out one person.

He said, "I don't need any reason."

I said I wanted to speak to his supervisor to see whether he was correct.

Immediately enraged, he said, "You're fuckin' right, we'll see."

He directed me to a designated area about thirty yards away, and he waited at the gate while he called someone. I had observed that the military police required drivers to open their car trunks, hoods, and doors. I got out of my car and stepped toward the trunk area.

The soldier shouted at me. "Get back in your car." I turned around and walked back the few steps I had just taken. He shouted again. "I have a better idea. Put your hands against your car and spread your legs."

My words at the checkpoint had made this soldier's blood boil. His instinctive action was to apply physical force. He patted me down, over all my body, and ordered me to keep my hands against the car, all because I had spoken words, asking his reason for stopping me.

A low-ranking soldier-supervisor arrived, and he and the MP concocted the false story that "because you refused a search" of your car, "you can't work at West Point anymore, and I'm escorting you off the post."

I insisted on seeing the provost marshal, a lieutenant colonel who was the head of the MPs. I drove to the MP building and sat waiting on a bench in the lobby. The next fifteen minutes saw four or five MPs gather and eventually surround me in a semi-circle, my back against a wall. They began to harangue me. The biggest talker said repeatedly, "You refused a search."

Others, like robots, asked, "Why did you refuse a search?"

Their chatter, like parrots, became absurd, but their overt physical coercion might not have been as dangerous to me and the country as their rapidly forming conspiracy to fabricate a lie. It took only minutes for at least six or seven of these military police soldiers at the gate and inside their own building to allege that I had refused a search at the gate.

The soldiers in the US military do not learn to solve problems without resorting to orders and coercion, including violence, and the same is true of the cadets at West Point and the students at the Naval and Air Force academies. About a mile north of the military police building are the cadets' barracks (dorms), which are exceedingly dangerous places for women cadets. The MPs' treatment of one civilian employee might be an anecdote, but the pervasive sexual assault of women illustrates a pattern of sexual and physical abuse at the military academies. As with suicide prevention, the Pentagon has spent hundreds of millions of dollars in its fruitless attempts to reduce sexual assault in the military, by soldiers on soldiers, cadets on cadets, with no improvement.

Military leaders attribute the failure to the nature or ignorance of service members, and never to the dysfunctional relationships that stem from the controlling behavior to which many officers of all ranks aspire. For years, the military academies recited two reasons for the increasing number of reported sexual assaults. The first was that the academies held themselves to higher standards and were, therefore, more aware of sexual assaults than other colleges. The second was that comparing the military academies with civilian colleges is like "comparing apples and oranges." This reasoning seemed ridiculous because all you'd need to do is compare the rate of sexual assault at the military academies with the rate at civilian colleges to determine whether the academies produced a higher rate of sexual assaults.

Thinking that surely the academies or the Pentagon had conducted a relevant study, I began a preliminary inquiry. I found nothing and, after more extensive research, I discovered there was no Pentagon study—at least not one available to the public—that compared the rate of sexual assault at the academies with the rate at civilian colleges. Then, using the Pentagon's own congressionally mandated studies of sexual assault and a study by the US Bureau of Justice Statistics on sexual assaults of students attending civilian colleges, I made the comparison in 2020.

The finding is shocking. The studies show that women military students are at serious risk of sexual assault on the grounds of the academies, beginning on the very first day in July of their first year, when they begin the equivalent of basic training and when most of them are a few days or weeks removed from high school graduation. In a 2020 book, *The Cost of Loyalty: Dishonesty, Hubris, and Failure in the U.S. Military*, I explained the comparison this way:

> The U.S. Bureau of Justice Statistics, part of the Department of Justice, estimated in its most recent study on the issue that the average annual sexual assault rate between 1995 and 2013 of female college students (all postsecondary, ages eighteen to twenty-four) was 6.1 per 1,000 women. The academies enroll about 12,900 students (a large majority of them between the ages eighteen and twenty-three) each year, and about 3,200 of them, or 25 percent, are women. [Based on the Pentagon studies, most recently in 2019] the current sexual assault rate of women attending the military academies is 32.2 per 1,000 women.[100]

A woman student at the military academies, with 32.2 assaults of women per 1,000, compared with 6.1 per 1,000 at civilian colleges, is over five times more likely to suffer sexual assault. (A Pentagon report, from 2023, covered the 2021–2022 academic year at the academies and "found the number of student-reported assaults at the academies had jumped 18% overall compared to the previous year—making it the highest number of sexual assault incidents since the Defense Department began tracking them in 2006," according to a report by ABC News).[101]

One indicator that such abuse has been normalized in the military is that victims believe they have no right to complain or that complaining will be futile or met with retaliation. In 2019, one of West Point's high-ranking officers and his wife explained to me the details of what had occurred inside the officer's academic department a few years earlier. At receptions and social events, the head of the department, an army colonel, after drinking alcohol, would approach women civilian professors and the wives of military officers assigned to the department. He would stand behind the officers' wives, hold their shoulders, and whisper "I love you" into their ears while their husbands watched, according to the officer and his wife.

The military husbands did not protest or report the colonel because he was senior to them or longer in rank, and, as the deputy head and later the department head, he had much additional formal authority over them. He controlled the courses they taught, the time of day they taught, the extra duties they would be assigned, when they could take leave with their families, whether they would be promoted, and what awards they'd receive on their retirements.

The colonel's behavior continued for years, until a civilian professor who was a subject of his advances complained. The obedience-ethos and conformist practices in the US military are so powerful that the military officers in the department, all of them with master's or doctoral degrees and many years or decades in the army, including service during the wars with Afghanistan and Iraq, learned to tolerate abusive behavior, or more precisely, feared speaking up on behalf of their wives because doing so could harm their careers. Their wives were silent because they knew that a complaint would hurt their husbands. When I asked why the officers and wives tolerated the colonel's behavior, both the officer and his wife said, "Everyone was scared."

The mental process that leads to such fear and silence was explained to me by one civilian professor who was the subject of an investigation for allegedly speaking inappropriately to cadets at West Point, the professor with twenty years' experience noted above. "I feel like I have done zero wrong. I haven't made over-the-line or borderline comments. It is kids that just feel they can bully faculty to get a better grade. In the end, because my department head [an army colonel] and I do not have a good relationship I'm certain he will recommend that I do some training of some sort. It is exceptionally frustrating but I'm just ready to submit and move on."

THE EXTENSION OF VIOLENCE TO EVERYTHING

Though many incidents could be cited, three of them illustrate how fear and silence inside closed organizations lead to the most serious consequences. In 1968, at My Lai, during the Vietnam War, a platoon of US Army soldiers killed over five hundred Vietnamese civilians, most of whom were women and children, and many of whom the soldiers raped before killing. In attempting to conceal what has become known as the My Lai massacre, the army whisked the platoon commander, Lieutenant William Calley, who personally killed over one hundred civilians, back to the United States.

Eighteen months later, after receiving a tip, an investigative reporter, Seymour Hersh, found Lieutenant Calley at a safehouse at Fort Benning, Georgia. Hersh's reporting revealed the killings at My Lai, for which he received a Pulitzer Prize. Despite the five hundred deaths, the army convicted only one soldier of a crime, Calley, and he served only three years of house arrest.

During the first year of the US war in Iraq (2003–2011), US Army soldiers ran a prison in Abu Ghraib, in which they humiliated and tortured Iraqi prisoners, including threats to execute them and forcing them to lie naked with each other. The abuse was depicted in photographs taken by the soldiers. In 2004, CBS and, again, Seymour Hersh, independently, revealed the soldiers' behavior at the Abu Ghraib prison.

In 2015, during the US war in Afghanistan (2001–2021), army soldiers in an airplane gunship, believing they were firing at their Taliban enemy, repeatedly circled a hospital in Kunduz and killed forty-two doctors, nurses, and patients, as referenced above. Top army generals exonerated all the soldiers and officers of criminal liability, using the rationale that the soldiers did not *intentionally* kill civilians. That's a lot like false advertising, in which a company asserts that its chemicals are safe because they do not lead to broken bones while not addressing the more relevant matter of whether the chemicals cause cancer. The issue the generals should have addressed was whether the soldiers acted with a reckless or negligent mental state when they killed the civilians, which, if so, would be a criminal homicide.

Since the 2020 publication of *Cost of Loyalty*, a book in which I described how the 15-6 report into the killings at Kunduz was incomplete, an army general officer who knew the details of the investigation about the forty-two deaths at the hospital contacted me to say that my analysis of what happened, the dubious near-total exoneration of the soldiers, was correct.

Hersh, the investigative reporter who revealed the incidents at My Lai and Abu Ghraib, contacted me to say that the book "perfectly" captured the culture of the US military and wondered about my safety at West Point.

An army major general, Antonio Taguba, after CBS and Hersh reported the soldiers' torture of prisoners at Abu Ghraib, was ordered to investigate and produce a report on what had happened at the prison. Taguba's report was critical of soldiers and officers at Abu Ghraib and of the army, and Taguba's honesty led to the end of his career. In 2007, Taguba told Hersh, and, years later, he told me the same story, that he was riding in Kuwait in the car of General

John Abizaid, who was the US commander of Central Command, which oversaw the wars in Afghanistan and Iraq.

"You and your report will be investigated," Abizaid warned Taguba.

Taguba said, "I'd been in the Army thirty-two years by then and it was the first time that I thought I was in the Mafia."[102]

Taguba's reference to the Mafia repeats a theme among anyone who works inside the military or other controlling institutions: anticipate retaliation if you dissent from any point made by someone higher in rank or identify problems in the institution.

Another army general officer once contacted me to say that he had finished a second reading of *Cost of Loyalty*. Near the end of our conversation, he said that he had been talking with a retired army officer who was his friend and later had held a civilian position in a presidential administration. The general officer half-laughed when he said it, but he wanted me to answer his question.

"I've got to tell you," he said. "We were wondering why you're not yet floating face down in the Hudson River?"

"I'm fine so far, general, and continue to stand guard on your behalf," I joked. He appreciated the humor and said goodbye.

Silence leads to uncertainty because, without communication, people cannot build alliances. "Uncertainty breeds loneliness in a fairly predictable emotional progression. Any experience of uncertainty makes us feel vulnerable, because if we don't know what's coming, we don't know if we can handle it. Feeling vulnerable in turn leads to anxiety, our biological response to threat. Anxiety tells your body to prepare to fight or flee," according to Professor Jeremy Nobel.[103] Without the resources to fight allegations or the wherewithal to speak up, people collapse, emotionally, mentally, physically, and existentially.

DECIDING WHETHER TO SPEAK UP

In 2025, the Pentagon's civilian leadership, part of the new Trump administration, banned diversity, equity, and inclusion (DEI) policies and programs and prohibited the military academies from using an applicant's race as a basis for admission. West Point's senior military officers' response went far beyond any new requirement. These officers, the superintendent, academic dean, vice dean, and department heads, began by banning books, courses, and teaching certain topics (such as any mention of climate change). One senior military officer told me they called their behavior "radical compliance."

The fear and silence induced by the new censorship became ingrained in professors' psyches. In the way someone experiences Stockholm syndrome, where hostages adopt the viewpoints of their kidnappers, one civilian professor said that censorship prevents professors from saying something that might get them in trouble.

"What?" I asked.

The censorship is "protective," he said.

Another professor, despite a new prohibition on her work, made the same argument, concluding, "I trust that the military officers are trying to protect us." The next day, those officers eliminated the academic major in which the professor taught.

The military administrators required the history department to eliminate teaching about the internment of Japanese American citizens during World War II. An army general, John L. DeWitt, had organized their internment.

The Dean's Office and every academic department examined professors' syllabuses to determine whether they contained any newly prohibited topics, words, or expressions. According to a *New York Times* report, the "U.S. Military Academy's leaders initiated a school-wide push to remove any readings that focused on race, gender or the darker moments of American history, according to interviews with more than a dozen West Point civilian and military staff."[104]

One civilian philosophy professor, Graham Parsons, in a May 2025 essay in the *Times*, explained why he would resign in protest at the end of the semester.

> In a matter of days…West Point abandoned its core principles. Once a school that strove to give cadets the broad-based, critical-minded, nonpartisan education they need for careers as Army officers, it was suddenly eliminating courses, modifying syllabuses and censoring arguments…. Cadets are told constantly that they are to lead a life of honor, to choose the harder right over the easier wrong, to have moral courage. But now they are learning that these are just empty slogans. What actual leaders do, it seems, is whatever protects their jobs…. West Point is abandoning its neutrality and jeopardizing a critical component of the very constitutional order that the military exists to protect…. Whatever else happens, it will forever be known that when the test came, West Point failed.[105]

The military administrators began an investigation of Parsons, but told him they would end their investigation—for his writing the essay without their approval—if he resigned immediately. Like the other professors, Parsons resigned. On hearing of the resignation, Secretary of Defense Pete Hegseth wrote, "You will not be missed Professor Parsons."[106]

An American political scientist professor, Timur Kuran, described in a now classic 1991 article how speaking and expression led to the collapse of the communist countries in Eastern Europe. "This simple framework offers a reason why a person may choose to voice a demand for change even when the price of dissent is very high and the chances of a successful uprising very low. If his private opposition to the existing order is intense and/or his need for integrity is quite strong, the suffering he incurs for dissent may be outweighed by the satisfaction he derives from being true to himself.... And because of the high value they attach to self-expression, they are relatively unsusceptible to social pressures."[107]

On the day Professor Parsons returned his work computer and identification card and left West Point, another professor, the one who had told me he found censorship to be protective, deferentially approached his (and Parsons's former) military supervisor, an army colonel. The professor, and an officer manager who accompanied him, confirmed that Parsons had departed, though some of Parsons's personal books remained in his old office. The professor, who had been Parsons's friend and colleague for over a decade, told the colonel, "I'm going now to urinate on his books."

Finding this kind of insult in the Soviet bloc countries, Professor Kuran wrote, "The typical East European feigned opposition to the few dissidents, though in private he applauded their mission. [The author, dissident, and last president of Czechoslovakia, Vaclav] Havel suggests that this admiration was coupled with a resentment: people who lacked the courage to be true to themselves felt threatened by displays of integrity on the part of others. They thus treated open defiance 'as an abnormality, as arrogance, as an attack on themselves, as a form of dropping out of society.'"[108]

During the spring of 2025, after a large meeting of faculty members, I left a building to walk back to my office in another building when an officer caught up with me from behind. He said, "You don't know me, but the reason I attended the meeting today was to hear you speak."

We walked a couple of hundred yards together and were about to separate to go to our respective office buildings. But he wanted to talk more and walked with me inside my building. Immediately on opening the door, however, the officer shortened his paces and walked more slowly down a hallway, lagging slightly behind me. I knew why because I had witnessed the same behavior in frightened army officers many times over the years, wanting to tell me what they believed but not wanting to be seen talking to me.

The officer was looking down the hallway and saw his future department head and deputy head, who were both army colonels, directly on our line. I understood his trepidation and subtly tried to say goodbye. The officer stayed with me, and we walked past his superior officers, who both noticed and side-eyed him and me. We walked past them and stopped outside their hearing distance, and he tried to show them by his quick departure that our conversation had been superficial.

In a rush, he told me, "I know I can get in trouble for being seen with you, and I should have walked away."

He spoke like he was a spy in the enemy's capital city, trying to leave his information without being seen. "I thought about walking away from you, but I decided not to do it."

"Thanks," I said, and he walked away.

A 2025 report by the Scholars at Risk Network, an organization that measures the level of academic freedom at colleges, noted a decline in freedom of expression around the world, including in the United States. The report defined academic freedom as "the human right to acquire, develop, transmit, apply, and engage with a diversity of knowledge and ideas through research, teaching, learning, and discourse."

The report, noting a "global crisis for academic freedom," found, "Even in societies that have long had strong and stable democratic institutions, elected officials with autocratic impulses are using both the levers of democracy and extralegal administrative measures to undermine democratic institutions, including universities."[109]

In *Fahrenheit 451*, a 1953 novel by Ray Bradbury indicating the degree at which books will burn, the firefighters in America, instead of stopping fires, were responsible for burning objectionable books, about as ignoble an act as banning books from a college library. While colleges are places of experimentation and discovery, I observed at West Point the behaviors that Scholars at Risk found accompany threats to freedom of expression: coercion and intimidation, travel restrictions, investigations and interrogations, and punishment, including termination.[110]

In addition to banning books from the library and phrases from syllabuses, West Point's senior military officers created a new rule that required professors to obtain their approval before writing or speaking in public, a demand to which I could not agree. A professor or writer who complied with such a rule could not be credited with writing or speaking according to his or her conscience. As a result, in September 2025, I filed a lawsuit in federal court, the Southern District of New York, against the top officers at West Point. I alleged that military administrators were infringing on my and the other professors' freedom of expression and academic freedom, in violation of the First Amendment.

I made this decision for the reasons expressed by the twentieth-century physicist, Richard Feynman, who shared the Nobel Prize in Physics in 1965. In his address to the 1974 graduating class at the California Institute of Technology, Feynman emphasized the importance of searching for truth. In his final words to the graduates, he said, "So I have just one wish for you—the good luck to be somewhere where you are free to maintain the kind of integrity I have described, and where you do not feel forced by a need to maintain your position in the organization, or financial support, or so on, to lose your integrity. May you have that freedom."[111]

Three days after I filed the lawsuit, I was sitting alone amid hundreds of cadets, staff, and faculty members in a large auditorium and waiting for the NATO secretary general, Mark Rutte, to give a presentation. The officer who had walked with me months earlier, somewhat reluctantly when we passed his superior officers, slid into my row and sat down, with one empty seat between us. A fellow officer was next to him, and the first officer said to both of us, "I shouldn't be sitting this close to you, but I'll do it."

"I appreciate that," I said.

Again, to both of us, he said, "We saw your lawsuit. No disrespect to civilians, but it took a civilian professor to do what officers should have done."

The event ended, and everyone stood to leave. The officer who was sitting a seat away from me said "thank you" and shook my hand. He and his fellow officer morphed into the crowd, too fast and far away for me to walk out with them.

In March 2025, a retired air force pilot, Lieutenant Colonel Ryan Sweazey, who, while on active duty, had spoken up and suffered for it described what a dissenter will encounter. "You see, in the United States military, every service member is willing to sacrifice their life for their country, but *very* few are willing to sacrifice their career. This means that if you are outed by the institution, most people will not hunker down with you when the rounds are incoming, they'll instead run the frag pattern [saving themselves]. You will look to them to put their name to something, to raise *their* hand, to stand with you...and most will cower."[112]

As Sweazey found, service members will not publicly help their best friends if doing so jeopardizes their careers. They have learned that survival leads to tangible benefits, promotions, ribbons, patches, special status, and accolades for them and their families. Only a small percentage of soldiers ever deploy to what are considered combat zones, and very few of them ever see actual combat. Almost all military personnel have many more opportunities to serve their country and to do so with greater benefit to the nation by speaking up about what they believe to be effective or ineffective, correct or incorrect, right or wrong. But soldiers and everyone else working for the military have never seen anyone rewarded for speaking up. They know intellectually the benefits of free expression, but they've not enjoyed the enrichment of engaging in it.

Before deciding to speak up, you should recognize that there's little or no support for most dissenters, and there's no reward in contemplating how to become a hero. Your decision-making and acting should be consistent with your conscience, which is easy to say but, for almost everyone, very difficult to practice. You can find a few people who will do it, like Alexander Navalny, a Russian dissident and Kremlin critic. After being poisoned in 2020 by Russian agents and saved by German doctors, he flew from Berlin back to Moscow to inspire his followers and show his disdain for President Vladimir Putin. Once back in Russia, Navalny was immediately arrested. In March 2022, Russia sentenced Navalny to nine years in prison. In 2024, Navalny, forty-seven, died, or was killed, inside a frozen, modern Russian gulag forty miles north of the Arctic Circle.

Fear can be a rational response, and Navalny did not have enough of it before he decided to return to Moscow, which might be another way of saying he possessed great courage. Major General Taguba, who described soldiers' abuse of detainees at Abu Ghraib prison, knew of the fear inside the US military and described it as a Mafia-like culture. But he, too, did not realize the severity with which the military officer-progenitors of this culture will act against a good man, including one who reports the truth.

The truth might set your mind free, but consider not speaking up unless first you're willing to defend others around you who have confronted the slapping hand of retaliation or abuse. You can observe the costs of free expression and decide later whether you're willing to endure them when your moment to speak is at hand. Even when fear is commensurate with the present danger, most people do not act to protect themselves or others.

They learn, too late, that "the regret of inaction is tenfold the regret of action," wrote Garry Kasparov, the Russian chess champion and exile, in 2024, in commenting on the courage and death of Navalny, and the failure of others to support him.[113]

If your fear is too great, then it might be necessary to remain silent. If possible, work behind the scenes to help others who have a greater need to speak to soothe their consciences. Retain hope that your moment to speak might occur in the future.

Key Points

- Fear and silence prevent correct decision-making.
- Controlling behavior and micromanagement degrade everything.
- A dissenter should weigh the costs and benefits before speaking.
- There's no reward in contemplating how to become a hero.
- Speaking according to your conscience is exhilarating.

CHAPTER 5

APOCALYPSE NOW

(YOU CAN'T FEEL WHAT YOU DON'T BELIEVE)

One way to evaluate your judgment is to ask where you would be now if you had selected other people with whom to have your closest relationships. Despite needing other people, you might have made mistakes because you acted against your conscience, and while under the direction of someone else or the spell of a personal or professional relationship. General Harold Johnson experienced this when he was the US Army's chief of staff from 1964 to 1968, during the Vietnam War, and was "widely admired as an exemplary soldier and a man of inspiring decency and honor." He claimed later in life that his failure to inform President Lyndon Johnson (no relation) that America was losing or would lose the war in Vietnam was an error of judgment: "I made the typical mistake of believing I could do more for the country and the Army if I stayed in than if I got out. I am now going to my grave with that lapse in moral courage on my back."[114]

General Johnson's failure to do something so important and simple as to speak up to try to stop a war he believed could be lost seems incomprehensible unless it's true that most people will preserve their status, job, and identity at almost all costs. In this chapter, *Apocalypse Now* refers not only to the film about the Vietnam War but also to a moment of personal or moral reckoning—a point in time when the consequences of one's misjudgment become clear. The chapter highlights the internal struggle whether to act according to your conscience or defer, though a better word might be succumb, to external pressures, as illustrated by General Johnson's regret in not speaking up when he believed doing so would be good for the nation. In other words, how will you know what compromises to make?

Depicting fictional events in the Vietnam War, the film *Apocalypse Now* shows how people's fantasies or limitations, both ends of a spectrum, overwhelm their judgment. The critic, Roger Ebert, called *Apocalypse Now* "one of the greatest of all films, because it pushes beyond the others, into the dark places of the soul."[115]

Released in 1979 and again in 2001 with additional scenes, it was inspired by the novel *Heart of Darkness* (1899), by Joseph Conrad, about a European ivory trader who becomes a god-like figure in Congo. The film chronicles the 1969 journey of an American army captain, Willard, an assassin, on a patrol boat inching up the fictional Nung River during the war (1963–1975). Captain Willard tries to find a renegade army special forces colonel, Kurtz, hidden in Cambodia, to terminate him with "extreme prejudice."

On the way, Willard encounters army Lieutenant Colonel Kilgore, who orders an attack on a village to secure a beach he can use for surfing. Kilgore concludes, "Charlie don't surf."

Kilgore, who pulls off his shirt, says, "I love the smell of Napalm in the morning...that gasoline smell.... It smells like victory."

Back on the river, Captain Willard's crew members stop a suspicious-looking flat-bottomed boat carrying fish, mangos, and a goat. During a search of the boat, a girl sitting on a can moves, and they shoot the girl and the three men with her. A crew member looks inside the can and finds a puppy. The girl, not yet dead, moves. Captain Willard, joining in the carnage, shoots and kills her.

"I told you not to stop. Now let's go," Willard tells the crew members.

Willard survives a spear attack by indigenous, zombie-like mountain-dwelling people who protect and treat Colonel Kurtz like a god. Kurtz orders Willard not to leave his village, and, as a warning, beheads one of Willard's crew members.

Kurtz is a third-generation graduate of West Point who cannot bear living because the army will not fight as brutally as he believes it must to win the war. He tells Willard that he, Kurtz, should be killed, and, with a machete, Willard hacks Kurtz to death. For Willard, their new god, the indigenous people create a walkway to his old boat, and he leaves the village.

APOCALYPSE NOW

The purpose of describing the ethos of the US military has been to show how, if the institution with the greatest resources and most adulation cannot accomplish its missions, organizations, families, and relationships with less support can similarly decline or fail. Americans in World War II, including Rosie the Riveters and especially the soldiers, saved the world from tyranny. But, since then, something has been out of whack inside the US military, which has been unable to prevail in the wars in Korea, Vietnam, Afghanistan, and Iraq, over a period of eighty-one years.

Audiences see in *Apocalypse Now* a depiction of the unnecessary degradation of people, one American soldier, Captain Willard, killing another, Colonel Kurtz, for the benefit of America, an incongruity that cannot be reconciled. I've observed similar contradictions at West Point, the place where future generals are educated and the stated goal of the military administrators is to build leaders of character to win the nation's wars, an empty mantra, like being obligated to say good morning every day but ignoring the hurricane outside. Through the story ahead, you may recognize the same in your organizations, families, and relationships, something seeming to be right and level, but underneath or deep inside there's that feeling of unease and knowledge that much is off-kilter and on the current course cannot be repaired. Plentiful positive variables, abilities, attributes, and experiences are present, but the fundamental of falsity overwhelms them, producing incorrect decisions, but not enough courage among the decision-makers, like General Johnson, and any number of people you might know, to change, to risk something to make life better for everyone.

I saw the incongruity once again on an early spring day in 2024 and the consequences when people act against their interests or those of others despite feeling what they're doing is wrong. I drove my car north along the Palisades Parkway, parallel to the Hudson River. Through Highland Falls, I maneuvered through two gate checkers at West Point and parked on Thayer Road. Since its founding, West Point's graduates, after working in branches in the army, such as infantry and field artillery, return to West Point for two or three years to teach cadets before heading back to their branches.

The process is the same today: army officers with new master's degrees but no prior teaching, practice, or research experience in their academic disciplines returning to teach the new cadets, who, years later, as officers, will do the same. These officers-instructors comprise 75 to 80 percent of the faculty and teach about 85 to 90 percent of the classes. Cadets experience teaching methods that are rooted in the early 1800s. For example, the military instructors direct cadets to "take boards" during classes. Each cadet must then stand and write with chalk on a blackboard while the instructor walks around the room and comments, as well as he or she can, on whatever the cadets have written.

Cadets' faces are nearly flush with the blackboards, and they receive little meaningful feedback. This Thayer method, which was introduced by an army officer, an 1808 graduate of West Point who became its superintendent in 1817 and has a road named after him, consumes an enormous amount of time. In a more modern setting, cadets would be learning for an entire class period from an experienced teacher who is an expert in a discipline and was hired via a competitive, nationwide job search.

At 5:30 that morning, the superintendent led a cadre of officers on one of their periodic runs. The runs are sometimes mandatory, but even when not mandatory, the officers, in my view, will comply and participate to avoid social censure and out-casting. Loathing this purportedly team-building exercise, most officers conform to the norm, treated like children, trotting in the darkness behind the three-star general, himself a graduate of West Point, who learned to believe that he could induce goodwill and teamwork through an activity that most officers experience as punishment.

I walked to the academic area, down Reconciliation Plaza, a walkway dedicated in 2001 and designed to reconcile the people from the North and South, a monument to the Civil War. Who would have known the need for reconciliation 136 years after the war ended? Cadets were walking to and from classes, but not in their usual uniforms, matching pants, shirts, shoes, socks, backpacks, and caps, because it was Denim Day, the one day each year when they may wear unmatched blue jeans and T-shirts to signal their support for initiatives to stop sexual assault. Most cadets don't believe that wearing denim helps to prevent sexual assault, but they, too, have learned to conform to appear virtuous and avoid being alone.

I made my way to the library, Thomas Jefferson Hall, where, in 2025, the superintendent, under pressure from Secretary of Defense Pete Hegseth, reinstalled a huge portrait of Robert E. Lee, the West Point graduate and former superintendent of the world's preeminent leadership institution, as the senior military officers there call it, who rejected President Lincoln's entreaties and became the top military officer for the Confederacy during the Civil War. (The president of the Confederacy, Jefferson Davis, graduated from West Point in 1828.)

I went to the top floor of the library, the Haig Room, funded by a 1947 West Point graduate, Alexander Haig, who was an army general, supreme allied commander in Europe, White House chief of staff for President Richard Nixon, and secretary of state for President Ronald Reagan. But Haig is most well-known for his unsteady performance on March 30, 1981, the day John Hinckley shot and nearly killed Reagan. With the president's life in the balance while in surgery, Haig told a television audience from around the world, "I'm in control here, in the White House."

As described by the Association for Diplomatic Studies and Training, "Al Haig, Reagan's Secretary of State, committed a PR faux pas—and showed a glaring lapse in basic knowledge of the Constitution—by telling the press that he was in control while the President was in surgery."[116]

Haig might have been trying to reassure the world, but his desire to be perceived as in control was more important to him than recognizing the vice president's (Bush) authority in the absence of the president. It was in the Haig Room this day and the next when military officers from Ukraine lectured on how best to fight the Russians. The two main characteristics that helped save Ukraine from the Russian invasion that began in February 2022 were mental flexibility and adaptability, the officers stated repeatedly, as well as being willing to make decisions quickly. I attended many of the lectures, but the few other people present were cadets whose attendance was mandatory, several military officers who organized the lectures, and one or two other faculty members.

After the last lecture that day in the Haig Room, I walked to the building that housed my department and office and trudged up four flights of stairs. The two elevators had been inoperable since a storm flooded the building more than nine months earlier. When I reached the top floor, I walked past the courtroom, which is used for the trials of officers and cadets who have been accused of crimes. Seeing two armed military police soldiers near the entrance, I knew from past cases that a cadet or officer was about to be sentenced to prison and sent in transit to Fort Leavenworth, Kansas, a hint of the old West in the modern army.

I stashed my backpack in the office and went to the courtroom, where late in the afternoon, a cadet on trial, a military defense lawyer, and a military prosecutor were about to make their final arguments to a military judge, a lieutenant colonel in the army. It's not often, probably never, that a CEO of a company or a college president can order the prosecution of an employee or student and then fellow employees will defend and prosecute him and others will serve as his jurors and, if the verdict is guilty, sentence him to prison, as at West Point and in all the criminal cases in the military.

The judge disclosed during the proceedings that he and the defense attorney had worked once together in the same JAG Office (Judge Advocate General's Corps). Later, the judge told the prosecutors that he had forgotten to tell them that he had also worked with the defense lawyer's wife at that same army post. In this clubby environment, where everyone works for the same employer, there's that ever-present feeling of unease, a formal proceeding ordered by a general, presided over by a judge, with lawyers and jurors, witnesses and a court reporter writing the words that are spoken, and it looks okay at first blush, but somehow something doesn't feel right, like two people in a relationship who look good together but both know there's a big problem.

The cadet had pleaded guilty to indecent recording, a military crime with a maximum sentence of five years' imprisonment. The crime is defined as "knowingly recording the private area of another person" in a place where the person had an expectation of privacy. Over two and a half years, the cadet had hidden surveillance devices and secretly recorded about seventy cadets in toilet areas and showers, and, most seriously, according to a prosecutor, in the barracks (dorm) suite he shared with other male cadets.

The cadet's recordings were discovered when one of his suitemates saw a photograph of himself naked on one of the cadet's electronic devices. During a search, investigators found on the cadet's devices photographs and videos of other cadets showering and using the toilet. The video that depicted the most egregious offense, the prosecutor argued to the judge, was of the cadet's suitemate masturbating in the suite, the only place at the academy where he had any privacy, an argument for a longer prison sentence.

By all accounts, including his own, the cadet should not have been admitted to West Point. When it was his turn to argue to the judge, the defense attorney, a JAG army captain, said that the cadet was "emotionally and psychologically" unfit for admission. The attorney pleaded for a lighter sentence (twenty months' imprisonment) than that urged by the prosecution (twenty-five months) by claiming that the cadet was not wholly responsible for the recordings. The captain said the cadet had taken the ACT college admissions test so many times (not indicating the number) without achieving a score that would lead to admission that an officer in the West Point Admissions Office finally told him to stop taking the test and that he would ensure his admission.

Months earlier, at a faculty council meeting (of senior civilian and military instructors) in November 2023, the superintendent's senior advisor for character had presented a formulaic, anodyne description of the character program for all cadets and how the program deals with the admission of such low-performing students. The minutes of the meeting reflected the administrators' knowledge of the problem stemming from admitting what they consider to be at-risk cadets, generally unqualified applicants who are admitted because of racial identity, athletic ability, or parents who are military officers, while better applicants are rejected:

> [The senior advisor] addressed the challenge of accommodating diverse backgrounds of incoming cadets within the character development framework. He acknowledged that each cadet arrives with a unique character formed by their life experiences and upbringing. Additionally, [the Senior Advisor] emphasized the role of faculty members as mentors and guides in supporting cadets' character development journey and encourages collaborative efforts across departments to ensure a comprehensive and practical approach to character development at the Academy.

The upshot of this vague, cheery summary is that no matter how much intervention and how many resources West Point directs toward character development of at-risk students, those students generally perform more poorly and commit more wrongdoing than cadets admitted based on standardized tests, grades, and previous high performance.

During his statement to the military judge, the cadet, from a written script, summarized the major events in his life. In essence, when he was in high school, he knew he should not attend West Point but was influenced by others to do so. He said that he did not know his biological father. He said that he was uncertain about his sexuality when he was young and that his stepfather called him "gay" and "fag." The stepfather killed himself when the cadet was eleven.

The cadet said he did not know of West Point until an admissions officer contacted him. The cadet told the judge his grades and ACT scores were not high enough to gain admission, but he accepted a spot at West Point's Prep School as a conduit to admission. The prep schools at the three military academies are like a thirteenth year of high school, where at-risk students who are not qualified to be regularly admitted take remedial courses and are almost automatically admitted the next year.

The cadet and his attorney argued that, without West Point's recruitment of him, he would not have been placed in a stressful environment and gone on to make the recordings of naked cadets. The cadet said he wanted to become a pediatric nurse after he was released from prison, not realizing, and emphasizing his immaturity, that few medical practices would hire a children's nurse who might be classified as a sex offender.

In determining the sentence, the judge was constrained by the plea agreement, through which the prosecution and defense had agreed that the term of imprisonment would be between twenty and twenty-five months. After adjourning to deliberate, the judge, in the early evening, sentenced the cadet to twenty-one months of imprisonment. I left the courtroom and went back to my office, completed some administrative work, and stuffed my backpack to get ready to leave.

Down a hallway, I ran into an army captain who was returning to his office. An academic article of his had been accepted recently for publication, which is unequivocally a nice accomplishment for any teacher, and I told him congratulations, but he frowned. He explained that a colonel in his department admonished and was deciding on a punishment for him because the captain had spoken to a news reporter about the article without first having asked the colonel for permission to speak.

The demoralized captain continued to his office, and I walked past the courtroom. Earlier I had seen the cadet's mother in the hallway hugging her son, but she was gone by the time I got back, surely because she did not want to see her son shackled. The MPs had placed a belt around the cadet's waist. Two cords of about two feet each extended from the belt to the handcuffs around his wrists. Because he couldn't lift his arms, he had to bend over to scratch his forehead.

I walked down the four flights of steps and later, at my place, clicked through television stations before landing on a channel that shows movies twenty-four hours a day. I stopped clicking when I saw Captain Willard in his patrol boat heading up the Nung River. In the next scenes from *Apocalypse Now*, I watched Willard and his crew members land at the home of French expatriates and, later, back on the river after their boat was repaired, fighting off a spear attack by the local tribesmen who believed Colonel Kurtz was a god. Captain Willard then found Colonel Kurtz, the troubled army officer, and killed him.

I realized that, to some extent, in my quarter century working at West Point by then, I had observed a modern *Apocalypse Now*. The interpersonal degradation might be acceptable, or at least somehow justifiable, if the military had won all its recent wars, instead of none of them, or if the military's high suicide rate could be attributed to the enemy and not to the near obsession of senior officers to control everyone around them, in my view. Once in a large meeting, a superintendent attributed a rash of cadet suicides to the their "preexisting conditions," not to any kind of malign treatment or influence they had experienced at West Point.

Once a cadet absconded with a rifle and a cartridge and used them to kill himself in a West Point building, but he was not found for days.

Another time, a lieutenant colonel who was a fellow faculty member hanged himself in a closet over the weekend in the building across the street from mine and was found by a custodian on Monday.

In another case, twenty-three years earlier, I had seen different MPs outside the courtroom shackle a military officer who was also on his way to imprisonment (seven years) at Fort Leavenworth for sexually assaulting a fellow officer's daughter, who was staying with his daughter on a sleepover.[117]

Regarding the cadet who recorded his classmates, the Decision-Making Formula shows that the decision to admit him was incorrect.

> If (natural abilities + attributes of success) + (observations/practices) > (fundamentals of failure) = correct decision-making.

In the first parenthetical, the cadet's low test scores showed that he lacked the ability to succeed. Regarding the attributes of success (HEFT), the cadet lacked humility, in that he thought he could get away with secretly recording naked cadets, and he lacked empathy, in that he did not realize or care how his actions would affect other people. In the next parenthetical, observations and practices, the cadet, on the cusp of imprisonment, seemingly still not grasping the gravity of what he had done, believed he could work in the future as a pediatric nurse, an unlikely job for someone convicted of indecent recording.

A FALSE CLAIM OF VICTORY

Relatively few people would expect that the courtroom at West Point would be open from time to time to house the criminal trials of cadets and officers working at what they are told by high-ranking officers is the world's preeminent leadership institution. You, too, might be disappointed when the positive way your family, business, or company is perceived does not match what you know is happening to you and people on the inside. Like those others watching from the outside, President Trump indicated in his May 2025 graduation speech at West Point that its attractive buildings and landscaping represent what is considered to be a notable institution.

He said, "This is a beautiful place. I've been here many times going to high school, not so far away. Good, a good place. Also, a military academy. Not quite of this distinction." (Trump attended the New York Military Academy, a private high school about eight miles north of West Point.)

Repeating a popular misconception, and troubling for a nation when it is lodged in the mind of the commander in chief, Trump told the cadets, "You could have gone anywhere. You could have gone to any school. This is one of the hardest schools to get into."

That misconception leads the president and other Americans into believing that he is receiving advice from generals who were some of the top students in the country when, in fact, the generals were very likely to have been unexceptional students. The military academies accept over 50 percent of the students who apply. But they report to Congress and the public, falsely, that their acceptance rate hovers around 10 percent.

The academies count as an applicant everyone who completes a "candidate questionnaire" online or attends a summer camp. They also count anyone on whom they have "started a file." That is, a high school student might not have completed any form, but West Point will consider the student to be an applicant if one of its admissions officers compiles data on the student.[118]

But the US Department of Education, to which the academies report their admission statistics, defines a real applicant differently: "Applicants include only those students who fulfilled all requirements for consideration for admission and who were notified of one of the following actions: admission, non-admission, placement on a wait list, or application withdrawn (by applicant or institution)."[119]

For the graduating class of 2016, which entered in 2012, West Point reported to its board of visitors, which includes members of Congress, that it had 15,170 "applicants" and "accepted" 1,339 of them. Had that been correct, which it was not, its acceptance rate would have been 8.2 percent.[120]

When not counting files started, candidate questionnaires, and summer camp visitors as representing applicants, West Point's actual number of applicants, those who were "fully qualified and nominated," was 2,394. West Point accepted 1,358 of them. Its actual acceptance rate was 56.7 percent.[121]

In 2025, a former air force officer, Trisha Dach, who graduated from the Air Force Academy and runs an admissions consulting business, described how West Point creates the appearance of a low acceptance rate. Dach wrote, "The West Point Acceptance Rate originates from the total number of applicants that start files with the West Point Admissions team.... From a recent class profile [the graduating class of 2027], this totals 11,430. Since only 1,255 were admitted, this leads the public to believe that the admissions rate was 11%. In reality, only 1,788 were qualified academically and in physical aptitude according to the admissions team. This results in a much higher acceptance rate of 70% if you are qualified."[122]

Dach's conclusion was, indeed, correct. In May 2022, a top military officer, the number-two person in the West Point admissions office, told the faculty council, "Applicants are candidates that have completed the candidate personal data record…or the initial application…. This is how we define applications."

He said that the "number of fully qualified" applicants to West Point is "typically about 2,000 each year. Of that 2,000, we might offer [admission to] 1500 applicants," an acceptance rate of 75 percent.

But the US Department of Education, on its College Scorecard for 2025, reported that the acceptance rate at the United States Military Academy was 14 percent.[123]

> Every moment that someone devotes time trying to appear to be something he or she is not leads the person to conform to the expectations of others. This reactive thinking, lacking in adaptability and spontaneity, makes it very difficult to know what to do when confronted with an emergency. This person might lapse automatically into thinking that someone else will tell her what to do, but she'll eventually realize she is alone and has not developed the capacity, independently, to make a correct decision or choose a few good options among very many.

In the following emergency, for instance, consider the large amount of knowledge and mental acuity you would want to have in determining how to make a correct decision about whether to kill another person. You'd have a lot more confidence in the decision-maker, perhaps yourself someday when considering end-of-life matters, if you knew that he had spent less time while a student at West Point looking over his shoulder and thinking constantly about how to avoid punishment for violating conformity standards and more time on how to make a correct decision in an emergency that might arise in his job.

During the war in Afghanistan, a captain in the army was back at West Point visiting and described to me how he had to decide whether to try to kill a Taliban fighter who was fleeing with an infant hostage. The captain and some of the soldiers under his command had been battling Taliban fighters who fought from inside a mosque and used child hostages to suppress the US soldiers' attack. Finally outgunned and with few men remaining, the fighter emerged slowly from the ramshackle mosque so the captain could see him holding a child to his chest with one arm. With his other arm, he fired an AK-47 rifle wildly in the soldiers' direction as he backed away and toward an escape into an urban abyss.

The US soldiers stopped firing and waited for the captain to tell them what to do. He knew that the rules of engagement permitted him to fire at the Taliban fighter, but there was no rule to tell him the likelihood that a bullet from his M16 rifle would hit the child and how much risk he should take that she would be killed. In position, like his soldiers, the captain did not delegate the decision to any one of them.

The Taliban man walked backward, and the captain had a second or two more to decide whether to fire before the man escaped with the child into the city. The captain explained that this was the most difficult situation he had encountered in the war, but his tone and demeanor indicated that he could or would not speak further about what he had decided: to fire to try to kill the Taliban fighter or allow him to escape with the child, or whether anyone had been killed.

Some might say that, given human creativity, I could think of other alternatives if I had been in the captain's shoes in Afghanistan. After all, most confident people believe that's what they've learned, problem-solving, in business and other schools, jobs, and relationships, and through any number of educational, experiential, and interpersonal interactions. Their certainty, that there are alternatives, is correct in many circumstances, but not in the resolution of some of the most difficult problems.

Sometimes there is no one who can help you, whether in thinking or acting. You, alone, must select one of two options, and you will find it helpful to have a method through which to do it. The army captain, alone, knew how much his prior education and training and, at that moment, physical and mental fatigue would affect his ability to hit the target, the Taliban fighter, and not the child. Did his education and experience allow him to process instantly what would happen to the child if the Taliban fighter escaped with her? What if the fighter was a Taliban leader? This would increase the pressure on the captain to shoot and risk the child's life.

These kinds of life-or-death decisions, when correct, are the grist of success, but when incorrect they can lead to big losses. For example, a New York City police officer, Jeff Herman, was a witness at one of my first trials, a case in which a man, residing in his mother's basement, threatened her with his barking dog. Officer Herman testified that he arrested the mother's son. Herman and I got along well, though it was impossible not to like him—humble, empathic, fair, and trustworthy (HEFT).

I saw him last on one New Year's Day in the late 1980s. I was walking down Flatbush Avenue in Brooklyn, and he was on duty, sitting in the passenger seat of a police car. Sticking out the window, he said, "Hey, Counselor."

"Officer Herman, Jeff, great to see you again."

We shook hands and discussed our great success on the dog caper. Almost always smiling, he leaned back into the patrol car. I pulled away and walked to the subway.

On May 30, 1989, a man who had been charged with kidnapping and released a few weeks earlier was back at his partner's home, threatening her with a gun and trying to force her not to cooperate with the district attorney. Officer Herman and his partner responded. They approached the man, and he shot the woman in the back and then took aim at the police officers. He shot Herman twice. One of the bullets slipped through a gap in the side of Herman's bullet-resistant vest and hit him in the chest.

Strong and young, but mortally wounded, Herman fought in the hospital for four days before losing a lung and then dying at age twenty-five. After escaping and on the run, the man killed himself two days after shooting Herman. Had the man not been released on low bail in the first place, a mistake attributed to a prosecutor, he might not have killed Herman. Both the prosecutor and Officer Herman were my friends.

Conformity and control deaden the brain and would not have helped the prosecutor know the correct amount of bail or the army captain in Afghanistan know whether to shoot. In our quest for competence, our own and that of others, we should promote adaptability and autonomy and, as much as possible, avoid people who project the opposite: narrow-mindedness and a desire to be the center of everything, aspiring more than anything to control as many people as possible. If you see lost wars, bankrupt businesses, and sometimes broken relationships, the apocalypses of life, you'll find some people who did not have the mental or emotional humility, maturity, or judgment to succeed at moderately difficult tasks.

Key Points

- Find what fits you and pursue it.
- Find people who can help you identify what actions produce success.
- Don't take too long to decide anything and miss finding better people.
- Ask what led you to a place or person and whether you can do better.
- Quitting may be necessary: If so, do it quickly and move on.

CHAPTER 6

NO GOOD DAYS FOR FAILURE

(KNOWING WHO CAN SAVE YOU)

A meaningful event for some people is their high school class reunion because they see friends who have known them longer than anyone else. At any age, our classmates are the original historians of our lives and can remain as important to our well-being as the people who come later. It's especially important to identify everyone who can help you now and equally valuable to identify your top abilities and attributes to enrich your life before it's too late to change direction. The purpose of this chapter is to learn how to identify those salutary people and find a method to identify those top qualities in yourself.

Because we can't reach our potential unless we're in good health, two people to consider first are pathologist J. Robin Warren and gastroenterologist Barry Marshall, who were obscure researchers and colleagues in Australia, until, in 1984, they found that most stomach ulcers are caused by bacteria (*Helicobacter pylori*), not by "stress, alcohol or spicy foods," as doctors had believed for a thousand years.

In the decade following Warren's and Marshall's discovery, doctors, still certain of their traditional treatments for ulcers, did not believe that bacteria could invade the stomach, an idea that "was considered blasphemy," according to a *New York Times* report. Unaware of the stomach bacteria, pharmaceutical companies made drugs to treat the burning acids that were believed to cause the ulcers, when the companies should have been developing antibiotics. But Warren and Marshall, the researchers, were correct, and more than two decades later, for their work, they were awarded the Nobel Prize in Physiology or Medicine in 2005.[124]

The Nobel Prize in Physiology or Medicine for 2024 was awarded to two American scientists, Victor Ambros and Gary Ruvkun, whose discovery was also the result of intellect, persistence, and collaboration. According to the Nobel Committee that awarded the prize:

> They discovered microRNA, a new class of tiny RNA molecules [which carry genetic information] that play a crucial role in gene regulation.... MicroRNAs are proving to be fundamentally important for how organisms develop and function.... Ambros and Ruvkun's seminal discovery in the small worm *C. elegans* was unexpected, and revealed a new dimension to gene regulation, essential for all complex life forms.[125]

Worms are easier than humans to study because their small size and genome (genetic material in a cell or organism) is one-thirtieth that of humans. Ambros's and Ruvkun's research on microRNA can be used to treat heart disease and cancer, among many other deadly conditions.[126]

People like Warren and Marshall, the Australians, and Ambros and Ruvkun, the Americans, are not interchangeable. In 2021, a researcher from Iceland who was working at the University of Cambridge explained to me that a pathogen can be a bacterium or a virus that should not be inside our bodies. He described his research: how to find the bacteria that current tests cannot detect and develop antibiotics that bacteria cannot resist. He went on to describe his work in detail, and it seemed that, despite the findings on stomach bacteria in 1984, very few people have been motivated to conduct this kind of life-saving research, or, more likely, very few people have the ability to do it.

I asked him how many professors and researchers were working in his area. He said, "About two hundred—in the world," which in 2026 contained more than 8.16 billion people.[127]

Remarkably, we are dependent on relatively few people, whether old friends or new scientists, to help us along in life, even to survive. In 2023, researchers reported the prevalence of cancer-causing bacteria in our bodies. The surprisingly high mortality rate is probably known mostly by the people who suffer from the stomach cancer that is caused by bacteria called *Helicobacter pylori* (*H. pylori*). The researchers summarized the incidence of cancer from bacteria:

> Although cancer is generally accepted as a disease caused by genetic characteristics and environmental factors, it has been reported that the effect of microorganisms on cancer could be approximately 20% of cancers human beings suffer from.... At least 15%–20% of cancers are triggered by infectious agents; 20%–30% are associated with tobacco products, 30%–35% with diet, lack of physical activity, and/or energy balance disorder (obesity).[128]

Wash your hands. Microorganisms and infectious agents that enter our bodies lead to possibly four million of the ten million cancer deaths each year in the world.[129]

A 2024 study, focused on the death toll from antimicrobial resistance (AMR)—bacteria that can resist antibiotics—found that the "AMR burden is forecasted to increase to 1.91 million attributable deaths and 8.22 million associated deaths in 2050," more than 10 million deaths per year.[130] Until then, from 2024 to 2050, more than thirty-nine million people, primarily the elderly, may die from bacterial infections that are resistant to antibiotics.[131]

Before their stomach-bacteria discovery, Warren and Marshall were not outwardly special or extraordinarily accomplished, but their seemingly mundane research—looking through microscopes for bacteria on glass slides that contained slices of human tissue—probably helped to save unknown millions of people from significant pain and suffering. Warren and Marshall helped us because they applied to their work simultaneously all three of their individual positive variables in the Decision-Making Formula (abilities, attributes, observations/practices). Recall the formula:

> If (natural abilities + attributes of success) + (observations/practices) > (fundamentals of failure) = correct decision-making.

Consider, within the variables, what is your top ability (math, language, or perception) and attribute (humility, empathy, fairness, or trust). Recall from the introduction to this book what is Question #1 in human development: "Is there an ability threshold, beyond which more ability doesn't matter?" The answer was *no*.[132]

In a competitive world, emphasizing your top characteristics will be most beneficial. As to shortcomings, everyone can compensate for some of them because success is determined partly by spending more time on something.[133] One of those hard workers was Warren Buffet, who became the world's most prominent investor while working in a small office in Nebraska. Buffet bought businesses that were operated by the most competent executives, who are difficult to find.

Quoted for a 1988 article, Buffet explained his approach to business, much of which centered around openness and curiosity. "If we get on the main line, New York to Chicago, we don't get off at Altoona and take side trips. We also have a reverence for logic around here. But what we do is not beyond anybody else's competence. I feel the same way about managing that I do about investing: It's just not necessary to do extraordinary things to get extraordinary results."[134]

In looking for managers to run his businesses, Buffet wanted someone who was "likable, talented, honest, and goal-driven." He said that he wanted businesses that did not need capital investment and which produced above-average returns and a steady flow of cash. The goal seems simple, but Buffet said finding such businesses was liking "bagging 'rare and fast-moving elephants.'"[135]

The author of the article, Carol Loomis, described the variable that placed Buffet above others. He was successful because of one "incontestable fact: Buffett brings an immense mental brilliance to everything he does.... Buffett's intellectual power is totally focused on business, which he loves and knows incredible amounts about."[136]

One manager described Buffet's approach: "He is constantly examining all that he hears: 'Is it consistent and plausible? Is it wrong?' He has a model in his head of the whole world. The computer there compares every new fact with all that he's ever experienced and knows about—and says, 'What does this mean for us?'"

Another manager said of Buffett, who, at age ninety-five, retired at the end of 2025, "I talk to him about all the important aspects of my business. He's never negative and always supportive. He's got such a massive mind and such a remarkable ability to absorb information."[137]

THE ELEMENTS OF COMPETENCE

Many years ago, at a boarding house in a small town in Wisconsin, about a ninety-minute drive from Minneapolis, Minnesota, an infirm sixty-nine-year-old man was sitting and watching morning television and did not have access to top-flight decision-makers. He began to squirm and contort his body to try to make what was happening inside him go away. He stiffened, locked in place. His caretaker, a disabled man half his age, shook and shouted at the man. But at about three hundred pounds, the dying man was frozen into the soft foam of his easy chair like a boulder stuck in mud.

The devoted caretaker, his own chest heaving in fright, called the emergency telephone number, and an ambulance with its two-man crew arrived at the apartment of the boarding house. When people suffer a heart attack, the blood stops flowing to and from their hearts. They crinkle and stiffen and need someone to compress their chests, cardiopulmonary resuscitation. Nobody knows, or at least no one remembers, whether the ambulance crew performed CPR or used a defibrillator to try to shock the man's heart back to working condition. They got the man to the nearby hospital posthaste, but not in time for the physician and nurses to perform a miracle. When the family arrived at the hospital, the only remaining issue for the doctor was to obtain permission to shut off the breathing machine connected to the man, my grandfather.

Under these conditions, he was likely to die. "In 2021, of those [heart attack sufferers] who were fortunate enough to have a bystander call 911 and have emergency medical services come to their assistance, only around 9 percent survived long enough to be discharged from a hospital—a dismal number that has barely budged in decades," according to a physician, Helen Ouyang.[138]

Writing in 2024, Ouyang described a sixty-one-year-old man who, decades after my grandfather died, was immobilized by a heart attack and prone on the floor of his living room, but he lived much closer to Minneapolis. The man's wife, a nurse, performed CPR, but his heart remained stopped. Arriving with others to a chaotic situation at the house, a first responder helped shock the patient twice with a defibrillator, but the dying man did not react. The first responder remembered that, in some cases, he should call the University of Minnesota Medical Center before taking a heart-attack victim to the nearest rural or suburban hospital.

The medic made the call to the medical center and found that the dying man qualified for a new procedure, extracorporeal cardiopulmonary resuscitation, ECPR, but the hospital in Minneapolis was about a thirty-minute, screeching-ambulance-siren drive from the living room floor, too far away, too long, to save the man. Instead, the first responders strapped the man into their ambulance wagon and met the hospital's mobile ECPR truck, a moving hospital, at the halfway point. "As the clock ticked toward 30 minutes from when Sauer's heart stopped, the chance of his survival was dwindling rapidly to zero."[139]

The feet of the dying man, Sauer, had turned blue by the time he was hauled into the mobile hospital for ECPR, though just in time not to die. The doctor in the mobile hospital, using needles and wires, threaded a narrow tube, "garden-hose" like, through arteries and veins, sucking out blood, oxygenating it, and then pumping it back into his body and, most importantly, to his brain. Nonetheless, the man, for days, appeared to be dead. But he survived and was back at work within two months.[140]

Ouyang, the physician and associate professor of emergency medicine at Columbia University, knew well the importance of surrounding dying patients with the best available doctors. She described two physicians on the job:

> [Dr.] Yannopoulos is known as an ECPR wizard; when I watched him at work on a cardiac-arrest patient recently, his fingers danced between needles and wires and dilators and cannulas [the tubes through which the blood moves] with such grace and speed that they were a blur. But what he and [Dr.] Bartos can do in under five minutes can take other teams 20 minutes or longer, while also increasing the risk of complications.

A critical-care doctor explained how competent doctors help save lives: "Where the training really becomes necessary is the thousands of microskills that have to be done exactly right—where you place your hands, what that feel is and how you're specifically doing all those things."

Ouyang explained, "Experience matters profoundly" because "patients treated at centers that perform fewer than 10 ECPR procedures yearly have 64 percent lower odds of survival; for every 10-case increase, the odds go up 11 percent."[141]

The heart-attack patients above, one who survived and one who did not, illustrate our constantly precarious circumstances and dependency on smart, creative people. The concept behind ECPR, oxygenating the blood and returning it to the body, originated in the 1960s, but the mobile hospital in Minneapolis was not operational until 2022. "In Yiannopoulos's [ECPR] program, if patients with a shockable rhythm are started on ECMO [extracorporeal membrane oxygenation machine] within 30 minutes of collapse, there is a nearly 100 percent chance of reviving them, with their brain function intact. After 40 minutes, the survival rate falls to about half, and then to around 20 percent after one hour. By contrast, patients receiving standard resuscitation measures have essentially no chance of survival after 40 minutes."[142]

Saving lives is a team project. In any number of institutions, despite the expertise or top performance of doctors, nurses, and other staff members, a patient may perish from substandard treatment or conditions inside a hospital—especially bacteria. A 2007 study showed that an estimated ninety-nine thousand patients die each year after contracting infections (bacterial, fungal, parasitic, or viral) while being treated in US hospitals.[143]

Regarding the new ECPR, according to Ouyang, "Not only does the procedure itself require mastery, but so, too, does the care in the I.C.U. afterward—an ineffable art as much as a precise science. The first 48 hours can be especially tenuous, requiring meticulous bedside adjustment of machines and medications, as the patient teeters between life and death."[144]

In choosing doctors who could save your loved one, you would not base the selection on such irrelevant factors as height, weight, or ideology. By way of comparison, in trying to identify top military officers, for example, federal researchers in 2017 found, "More than any other single factor, intelligence...predicts success or achievement in learning, training, education, workplace performance, health, income, and wealth."[145]

Intelligence manifests itself in many ways, and you might not realize how truly competent you are because you're in a job or relationship where the circumstances do not permit you to access your top ability and attribute. Perhaps you've been doing something or with someone so long that you've lost the inclination or forgotten how to try something new, which might be where you could fully actualize your capabilities. Thus, ask what you can do best. Who brings out the best in me?

Daeyeol Lee, a professor of neuroscience, found that intelligence originates in the brain and is connected to the nervous system and is reflected in your "ability to solve complex problems or make decisions."[146]

Other researchers define intelligence more broadly, "as a general mental ability for reasoning, problem solving, and learning...[that integrates] cognitive functions such as perception, attention, memory, language, or planning." Intelligence "can be reliably measured by standardized tests with obtained scores predicting several broad social outcomes such as educational achievement, job performance, health, and longevity."[147]

Standardized tests' measurements of mathematical, verbal, and spatial (perception) proficiency help identify qualified people for colleges and jobs—from a physicist whose fingers write equations on a board to a carpenter whose fingers help to construct buildings. All things equal, if you can select only one criterion on which to select a physician, for example, intelligence appears to be the best one.

> Now might be the moment to sit back and think about which ability has served you best or whether you might not be using or optimizing your top ability. Are you working in a job that is somewhat comfortable and pays the bills but does not allow

> you to use your creativity? Perhaps you're a good employee and provider for your family because you're organized (math ability) and everyone trusts you. But your top ability might be verbal or perceptual and, along with your keenest attribute, empathy, you could be more successful if given the opportunity to lead people. What should you do if your partner or spouse does not recognize or help you develop your top ability, perhaps preferring the stability provided by a successful job or business to the uncertainty of acquiescing to your following your dreams, most of which turn out to be just dreams, though not always?

Given such natural considerations, it's wise to consider the opportunities that could arise if you optimized your strengths before it's too late. In recent years, however, many colleges, as well as companies, have deemphasized the traditional way, standardized testing, to find top students and employees with top abilities. Their goal is to create a student body and workforce where the identities of the members are proportionate to the composition of the general population.

Regardless of the criterion used to measure someone, and you might be the one who wants to use it, you should try to find the best way to predict how to obtain the most success or happiness or whatever intangible feeling you value most. This is especially important because, as noted in chapter one, people in the US die, on average, 3.5 years sooner than people in comparable countries. The conditions leading to shorter lives in the US might also be reflected in declining educational performance. For the incoming college class of 2023, students' scores on the ACT (American College Testing) were the lowest in thirty years.[148]

For the 2024 incoming class, students' scores on the SAT (Scholastic Aptitude Test) were the lowest since its scoring system was changed in 2016.[149]

The Nation's Report Card, the National Assessment of Educational Progress, by the US Department of Education, from 2025, showed that "the 67% of eighth-graders who scored at a basic or better reading level in 2024 was the lowest share since testing began in 1992," according to the *Wall Street Journal*.[150]

Overall, from 1990 to 2019, according to the Department of Education, high school graduates' grade point averages, which cannot be standardized given the multitude of different schools and teachers, increased from 2.68 to 3.11, a sign of grade inflation everywhere given the students' declining test scores over the same time.[151] The University of California now prohibits its colleges from considering standardized test scores in undergraduate admissions.[152]

Recall that you are trying to find your top ability and, in an emergency, the best doctor to treat your loved one, and that's becoming more difficult. A 2024 report in the *Washington Free Beacon*, for example, indicated that a new associate dean of admissions at the University of California, Los Angeles, Medical School, Jennifer Lucero, deemphasized both the standardized Medical College Admission Test and college grades and increased the use of race in determining whom to admit, which led to the admission of less qualified students than in previous years. The dean of the medical school, Steven M. Dubinett, responded to the *Beacon* article. "I consider it to be fact-free."[153]

According to the *Beacon* report, however, three years after Lucero, the associate dean, was hired, UCLA dropped from sixth to eighteenth place in *U.S. News & World Report's* rankings for medical research. Not disputing his medical school's rating decline, Dr. Dubinett, the dean, claimed that the drop in research might be attributable to the school's assigning more clinical duties to faculty members and their resultant lack of time with which to propose new studies and obtain research grants to complete them. Professors who spend more time than usual with students or in clinics is a sign that the new students need more help. This means, of course, that the UCLA faculty members will spend less time on research and will be less likely to produce as much knowledge as in the past, such as perhaps discovering new methods to combat bacteria.

The *Beacon* noted that "in some of the cohorts she [the associate dean] admitted, more than 50 percent of students failed standardized tests on emergency medicine, family medicine, internal medicine, and pediatrics…though only 5 percent of students fail each test nationally."[154]

One UCLA faculty member said, "UCLA still produces some very good graduates. But a third to a half of the medical school is incredibly unqualified."[155]

A patient's ability to identify a competent doctor who graduated from UCLA's medical school is made more difficult by UCLA's pass/fail grading system in its critical clinical clerkships. Its grading policy reads, "The Core Clinical Clerkships include Emergency Medicine, Family Medicine, Internal Medicine, Neurology, Obstetrics and Gynecology, Pediatrics, Psychiatry, and Surgery. The possible grades for each Core Clinical Clerkship are: Pass, Fail, or Incomplete…. A total evaluation score > 48% will result in a clinical performance grade of Pass. A total evaluation score of <48% will result in a clinical performance grade of Fail."[156] (In UCLA's grading scheme, above, we are left to wonder whether to pass or fail a medical student who scores exactly 48 percent.) Not many people would be confident in a surgeon who passed a course in, of all things, surgery, with a score of 48.1 percent.

The University of Minnesota Medical School, from which the extracorporeal doctors operate, created its own admissions controversy when it required newly admitted medical students in 2022, in a "white coat" ceremony, to recite an oath that deemphasized modern medical treatments. An associate dean, Dr. Robert Englander, directed the new medical students to take the oath, and he recited it with them on their first day at the medical school. The oath included the following:

> Our institution is located on Dakota land.... We commit to uprooting the legacy and perpetuation of structural violence deeply embedded within the health care system. We recognize inequities built by past and present traumas rooted in white supremacy, colonialism, the gender binary, ableism and all forms of oppression...[and] we commit to promoting a culture of antiracism, listening and amplifying voices for positive change. We pledge to honor all indigenous ways of healing that have been historically marginalized by western medicine.[157]

A group advocating free expression, the Foundation for Individual Rights and Expression, complained that such an ideological oath was a form of compelled speech and violated the First Amendment. Presumably recognizing that the claim was correct, the university's legal department said the oath was not mandatory.[158]

The irony of requiring or urging the oath was that, in "honoring all indigenous ways of healing," the Minnesota Medical School was, in effect, displacing newer medical practices. Even if everyone agreed with the oath's recognition of indigenous healing practices, because time is the most important resource—after forty minutes without modern treatment, a heart attack patient will almost surely die—the teaching or consideration of ineffective or less effective remedies distracts medical students and doctors from studying and practicing methods that are more likely to lead to life-saving interventions.

THE ORIGINS OF POOR DECISION-MAKING

Almost all experts in psychometrics (testing) believe that standardized tests, better than any other measure, predict how people will perform at school and in colleges and, later, in the workplace. A continuing issue for colleges and society, however, is that the scores of Black students, and to a lesser extent Hispanic students, on the tests remain significantly lower than the scores of Asian and White students. However, it turns out the tests can reliably predict for all students in every racial group who will succeed. The upshot is that if you have not experienced advantages available to other people, you can overcome disadvantages by finding, measuring, and acting on your top ability.

A Supreme Court decision in 2023 prohibited colleges from using race in their admissions decisions. This was despite a dissenting justice in that case relying on a broadly cited 2020 study that seemed to provide a compelling rationale to admit into medical school Black students specifically because of their race. The study found that infant mortality of newborn Black babies was lower when their physicians were Black.

The four authors, university researchers and professors, summarized their findings: "Results examining 1.8 million hospital births in the state of Florida between 1992 and 2015 suggest that newborn–physician racial concordance is associated with a significant improvement in mortality for Black infants. Results further suggest that these benefits manifest during more challenging births and in hospitals that deliver more Black babies."[159] In other words, the study showed that one condition, that a doctor was Black, increased the likelihood that a Black baby would survive.

The researchers believed that something they could not identify must have led to the lower mortality rates for Black babies who were treated by Black physicians. According to the researchers, "These results underscore the need for research into drivers of differences between high- and low-performing physicians, and why Black physicians systemically outperform their colleagues when caring for Black newborns."[160]

The researchers concluded that, because "it is clear that patient–physician racial concordance provides benefits," their study should lead to many new investigations and practices. "Hospitals and other care organizations [should] invest in efforts to reduce...biases and explore their connection to institutional racism," which "will also require raising awareness among physicians, nurses, and hospital administrators about the prevalence of racial and ethnic disparities, their effects, furthering diversity initiatives, and revisiting organizational routines in low-performing hospitals."

However, the researchers were concerned about one mystery in the study that they could not explain: "We find no significant improvement in maternal mortality when birthing mothers share race with their physician."

That is, if for some unidentified social/cultural/intellectual reason Black physicians provide better care to newborn Black babies than do other physicians, then Black physicians should also provide better care to the babies' Black mothers. But the researchers could not explain why Black physicians did not lead to better care (lower mortality) for the Black mothers.

At this point, the researchers seemed to wave away the anomaly they had identified. "Finally, we observe no effect of concordance on mortality for birthing mothers, suggesting communication is not the exclusive mechanism by which concordance benefits will manifest."[161] Faced with data that could challenge their conclusion, that Black doctors are best for Black babies, the researchers essentially stopped their inquiry and reported their findings.

As evidence would show, however—and the evidence was available to the researchers but they did not see it—their study was invalid. But before later researchers discovered and explained why the study was invalid, the study led to mistaken nationwide reporting.

CNN, in 2020, declared, "Black newborns more likely to die when looked after by white doctors."[162]

The *Washington Post*, in 2021, reported, "Mortality rate for black babies is cut dramatically when black doctors care for them after birth, Researchers say."[163]

When the US Supreme Court, in 2023, found that racial preferences in college admissions decisions were unlawful, Justice Ketanji Brown Jackson, in her dissenting opinion, referenced the researchers' 2020 study as a primary reason why racial preferences should be allowed to continue in college admissions. Justice Jackson wrote, "Beyond campus, the diversity that UNC [University of North Carolina] pursues for the betterment of its students and society is not a trendy slogan. It saves lives."

Referencing the study, from a legal brief submitted to the court, Justice Jackson wrote, "For high-risk Black newborns, having a Black physician more than doubles the likelihood that the baby will live, and not die."[164]

But given the flaws in the study—more precisely, the analytical error of the researchers—Justice Jackson's conclusion was unfounded. Different researchers, in 2024, found the 2020 researchers' analytic error. The 2020 researchers had failed to isolate the weights of newborn babies. Low birth weight (under 3.3 pounds) is the most important factor in predicting a baby's survival.

The reason that Black doctors appeared to lead to better care for Black babies was that White doctors were handling the most seriously ill newborns, those with low birth weights and who were most likely to die. Using the same data from Florida, the 2024 researchers explained how the 2020 researchers arrived at their erroneous conclusion, that Black physicians produced lower mortality in Black newborns:

> In fact, a crucial omitted variable is evident.... Because controls for the newborn's health condition are limited to only the 65 most common diagnoses across *all* births, there are no controls for a birth weight under 1,500 g [3.3 pounds]. Such 'very low' weights are an important predictor of mortality. In 2007, only 1.2 percent of White newborns and 3.3 percent of Black newborns had weights in this range; but these newborns accounted for 66 percent of neonatal mortality among White babies and 81 percent among Black babies.[165]

The 2020 study's "estimates of the impact of racial concordance on Black newborn mortality are substantially weakened and often become both numerically close to zero and statistically insignificant, once the analysis controls for the mortality effect of very low birth weights."[166]

The 2024 study, according to its authors, George J. Borjas and Robert VerBruggen, "shows how an important research design decision [by the 2020 researchers] can yield…[a mistaken] empirical finding of racial concordance in newborn mortality."

The Florida data showed that White physicians were treating the most seriously ill newborn Black babies in neonatal intensive care units. "It turns out that a disproportionately large number of Black newborns with very low birth weights are attended by White physicians. We show that once we control for the impact of very low birth weights on mortality, the estimate of the racial concordance effect is substantially weakened and becomes statistically insignificant in models that account for other factors that determine newborn mortality."[167]

According to a report about the 2024 study, "The sickest babies, the new study pointed out, are most likely to be treated in neonatal intensive care units (NICUs), which are largely staffed by white physicians. Just 3.8% of the nation's neonatologists are Black."[168]

One of the authors from the 2020 study, Aaron Sojourner, recognized the error and wrote on X: "Adding an omitted variable to the model in our…paper on physician-patient racial concordance changes the result. Grateful to Borjas & VerBruggen for continuing to advance the science."

In responding to the 2024 study, another author of the 2020 study, Brad Greenwood, wrote, "I am glad that there is a continued and robust dialogue in the scholarly community about the means by which the racial mortality gap in birthing outcomes can be ameliorated. It is important work that needs to be continued."

Errors occur when we stop looking hard for the truth. An economics professor, Theodore Joyce, wondered why the error had not been identified. "Why was the exclusion of the VLBR [very low birth weight] not discovered in the peer review process?"[169]

Joyce found five errors that led to the faulty study, including one that is especially disturbing because it suggests that truth can be overridden by scientists' emotions and political preferences. Joyce attributed three errors to the 2020 authors. Those errors concerned their research design and the possibility that none of the authors was a clinician, who presumably would have been quick to recognize the prevalence of low birth weight in infant mortality.

The other two errors were attributable to the peer reviewers of the study, who, for any number of reasons, did not recognize the faulty research design. (Professional peers must recommend articles before they can be published in most journals.) In addition, Joyce wrote, "Finally, the...article was published [two months] after George Floyd's murder and the ensuing national conversation around racial discrimination. Reviewers are only human, and these events may have affected how the results were interpreted."[170]

A psychology professor, Paul Bloom, in summarizing his skepticism about the flawed 2020 study, illustrated how anyone, for many reasons, might not fully recognize what is correct or true. "I wasn't surprised when I saw the re-analysis because I didn't believe the original finding. If your goal is getting things right, then the advice to be skeptical of findings that flatter your views...is just the thing. But what if your goal is to feel good about yourself? To persuade people to join your cause? To mock your ideological opponents? To make yourself popular within a group of like-minded individuals? Being skeptical about findings that support your view is great if you want to pursue the truth, but it is an awful strategy if you want to satisfy these other goals. For whatever it's worth, I believe that pursuing these other goals at the expense of truth, though understandable for individuals, makes the world worse."[171]

Research studies and standardized tests are methods to use in the search for truth. The tests, according to experts, are effective in predicting future performance.[172] There is some public consensus on this point in that a 2022 Pew Research Center survey found that 85 percent of respondents believed that standardized tests should be used in college admission (as a major factor, 39 percent, as a minor factor, 46 percent).[173] The point is that if you're not quite where you want to be, there's a way to find a better direction. While most of us will not want to take a test to measure our abilities, we can use our experience to decide to move in another direction and decide who should accompany us.

You'll want to use some method to do that, whether relying on top doctors to save heart attack patients, eminent scientists to eradicate bacteria, or classmates and friends to help shape your thinking. Recall Johnny, my high-school friend who seemed to live alone in a rickety old house in the country and was later imprisoned for various crimes. Few reasonable persons would credit his past adversity and use it as a basis to hire him for an important job.

I once ran into another character with similar issues who was an important witness on three murder cases that I prosecuted. Along with his childhood friends, he operated a lucrative cocaine and heroin-dealing operation out of bodegas, gritty inner-city convenience stores, in the Brownsville section of Brooklyn. They called themselves the Wild Bunch and killed at least eleven people, including local robbers who stole money from addicts before the addicts could enter their stores and purchase illegal drugs.

After he was indicted for murder, the man, Bostick (pseudonym), agreed to become a cooperating witness and testify against his old friends to avoid a sentence of life imprisonment. Bostick and I were both about thirty years old, and we communicated easily, or it seemed that way to me. At a break in one of the trials, we walked from the courthouse back to the district attorney's office, a few blocks away. Bostick, a prisoner himself because he was serving up to twelve years in prison as part of his cooperation and plea agreement, was always shackled and escorted by detectives. During the break, in an office area, I told him we could not speak about his testimony because he had not been cross-examined yet by the three defense lawyers who were representing three members of the drug operation who were on trial, including the boss.

But I asked Bostick how he was doing. He said he was doing okay, but I sensed he had something on his mind. I asked a couple more times what was wrong, but he resisted speaking.

In most circumstances, I would have stopped, but a murder trial is not a normal event. I asked again. Finally, smiling, Bostick lifted his chin and raised his chained wrists, like a preacher giving absolution to a sinner.

"Did you see that pretty brown lady in the courtroom?"

"No," I said.

Usually only a few people attend trials. But for this case, the Wild Bunch had filled the courtroom with its members.

Bostick seemed to make the sign of the cross, but I knew this couldn't be a genuine gesture because, from what I had observed, he had no religion. His shackles were clanging like large metal bowls and pans banging above a large industrial sink in the kitchen of a restaurant.

"That lady is my wife," said Bostick.

Stunned, I remembered I had not asked whether he was married because he had pleaded guilty to killing his *girlfriend's boyfriend.*

Realizing the gangsters had brought his wife to the trial to try to stop him from testifying or from testifying truthfully, I rushed to say, "We can relocate your wife. I'll get someone on the job right now."

"Did you see that lady next to her?" Bostick asked, ignoring me. "That's my wife's mother."

I cursed myself for not asking whether he was married. Despite the chains wound around his body, he had the upper hand as I pleaded with him to let me help his wife. Bostick would have none of my despair. He had requested bacon, egg, and cheese sandwiches, and I brought them to him in the mornings, and he didn't ask for much more than that. He seemed to want to spare me any more work. Like a preacher at a revival, he lifted his hands again, and the shackles rattled like a dying man taking his last gasps of life.

"Mr. Tim," he said, "don't worry about it." He hesitated and smiled. "That bitch hasn't come to see me in prison in years."

I froze, and Bostick smiled wider. We were silent. Despite having encountered a lot of severe people, I didn't know whether he was joking or telling me to move on and get him a sandwich for lunch. Bostick understood well his predicament in prison and knew that neither his wife nor childhood friends, who were on trial, were his allies. He knew he had done some bad things, and I knew he would not change.

In fact, both Bostick and Johnny, coincidentally, when in their sixties, were at the same time serving fifteen-year prison sentences for serious crimes. No matter their disadvantages growing up, you would not hire them to complete an important task, at least not without requiring them to take a relevant standardized test to measure their current honesty and ability. The takeaway here is that, unlike Bostick and Johnny, you can almost immediately take a new direction if you're able to identify and measure your potential and are willing to act to fulfill it.

Key Points

- You don't have to live with bacteria: find people who can help you.
- Some people will not change: be wary of them.
- Incompetence can be avoided by relying on your reasoning.
- Decide how to test yourself.
- Assess your abilities, attributes, and experiences: act on the best ones.

CHAPTER 7

HOW NOT TO HAVE A SHORT LIFE—HAPPINESS

(YOU'VE GOT TO GET OUT OF THE CHAIR)

In September 2022, Hurricane Ian devastated Florida's Gulf Coast, causing sixty people to drown, many in their cars, and destroying the mobile home and almost all the belongings of Martha Shaw, eighty-three, unmarried, a retired elementary school teacher. Her property insurance did not cover flooding, which, more than wind, most affected her home, and she lived in a shelter with her dog for over a year. Immobile, walking with a cane and needing a wheelchair for long trips, Shaw began to decline, her activities limited to sitting and playing puzzles alone at the shelter. One day, she told herself, "You've got to get out of the chair."[174] She did that and more, though her decision might have come sooner if someone had been there to help her.

Shaw realized that the greatest obstacle she faced was not the flood, but rather her isolation, which is more deadly. Isolation is the one fundamental of failure that can most easily prevent you from finding happiness, which depends on developing close relationships with other people. Though all of us appreciate solitary time, too much of it is not helpful, and, as Shaw found, isolation can afflict us only if we do not act. Indeed, in the first instance, inactivity is the fundamental of failure that leads to isolation, and, in this chapter, you'll see the importance of surmounting both of them.

The staff at the shelter encouraged Shaw to consider an assisted living arrangement. Instead, she used her remaining retirement money to build a house on cement columns, a requirement for new construction in the low-lying area, and she made the final payment—on a hurricane window—in cash, her resources drained. Understanding her need to act, Shaw, eighty-four by then, said, "I'm literally losing hair. And that's nothing but stress and worry."[175]

Togetherness was an evolutionary response to counter adversaries who would stalk our ancestors or steal their provisions. Loneliness conflicts with our nature; togetherness protects us.[176] With evolution often occurring over long periods of time, recent abrupt changes to our routines may be producing dramatic negative effects. A 2024 study noted "a profound shift in the setting of Americans' daily lives."[177] It showed, "On an average day in 2022, U.S. adults spent one hour and 39 minutes more time at home than they did in 2003. This translates to roughly 10 percent more time spent at home on a daily basis."[178]

Americans are more entrenched in their residences than in the past. The study's author, Professor Patrick Sharkey, found, "Over the period spanning from 2003 to 2022, there was minimal change in the overall time U.S. adults spent engaged in work, school, eating/drinking, leisure without a computer, sports/exercise, and religious/spiritual activities. However, the amount of time in each activity spent away from home declined and the amount of time in each activity spent at home increased. The shift in the location of these six categories of activities accounts for more than 70 percent of the overall rise in time spent at home."[179]

Sharkey believed that the reasons for spending more time at home ranged from increased use of technology to greater fear of appearing in public. But he cautioned that "the rise in time at home should not be interpreted to mean that Americans are simply retreating to their homes on their own, isolated from others. Spending more time at home is, in fact, associated with spending less time with friends, but it is also associated with spending more time with family."[180]

However, Sharkey's last point, about spending more time with family, requires a significant qualification that undercuts the reflexive conclusion that more time at home leads to a better quality of life or more happiness. In fact, it seems that people who spend more time at home are more likely than in the past to be spending the time alone. The US Census Bureau reported that "64% of households were classified as family households in 2024. This marks a significant change from 50 years ago, when 79% of households were family households" (where a household is defined by "at least one person related to the householder by birth, marriage or adoption"). Thus, it seems that when people leave their friends, assuming they have friends, they are returning home to a structure that is more likely than in the past to be empty, leaving them alone.[181]

Perhaps that's why Sharkey found that "activities conducted at home are associated with lower levels of happiness and are viewed as less meaningful." That might be partly because residents are alone, and not with family members. "Although additional evidence is needed to assess whether being at home has a causal effect on emotional wellbeing," according to Sharkey, "the strongly consistent findings using two very different analytic approaches provide more confidence in the relationship between the setting for activities and individual emotions."[182] In other words, more time at home appears to lead to less happiness.

People can feel alone when at home and when surrounded by others, as Martha Shaw found in the shelter as she planned to flee it and overcome her hurricane-induced abandonment, which is one of the five fears common to everyone, along with dying, mutilation, immobilization, and humiliation.[183] But the necessary act of moving from the shelter is probably not sufficient to eliminate fear, diminish isolation, or produce happiness. Whether in the home or elsewhere, isolation has become a significant factor in degrading mental health.

In a 2019 study, Cigna, an insurance company, found that loneliness was increasing. "Of a possible total loneliness score of 80, the current average loneliness score in America is 45.7, up from 44 in 2018. Loneliness is defined as a score of 43 or higher on UCLA's Loneliness Scale. Currently, 61% of Americans have a loneliness score of 43+, compared to 54% in 2018."[184]

The report found that "nearly four in 10 (38%) agree with the statement, 'I feel that I do not have close personal relationships with other people.' Additionally, one in three (34%) do not think other people respect their skills and abilities, and a quarter of Americans believe there is no one who shares their interests and concerns. Furthermore, how people feel about their personal relationships is a key driving force in how lonely they feel. For example, those who do not feel they have close relationships that give them emotional security and well-being have an average loneliness score of 57, nearly 15 points higher than those that do (42.3)."[185]

The report found that mental health affects loneliness more than physical health; men are lonelier than women; entry-level and senior executives are the loneliest workers; and remote workers feel more isolated and lonelier. But, fortunately, the primary remedy to loneliness is within your control: daily human interactions, including those on the job, where the most important working condition is flexible hours.[186]

A 2024 study described loneliness as a "distressing feeling" in older adults in which "the quality or quantity of their social connections does not meet what is needed or desired." The researchers' analysis confirmed the findings of many other studies: "individuals who feel lonely (versus not lonely) have a higher risk of developing dementia and other cognitive impairments," even when accounting for social isolation and clinical, behavioral, and genetic risk factors for dementia. Simply, the feeling of loneliness (one variable) contributes to dementia and cognitive impairment, according to the studies.[187]

Making loneliness more difficult to surmount is the overall mental health of people in the US, which appears to be declining. Researchers, in 2022, after surveying many studies, found, "Approximately 1 in 5 adults and 1 in 6 youth experience mental illness each year," with the rate increasing, and that "over 20 million Americans have a substance use disorder," costing workers and employers over $77 billion each year.[188]

Think of when you've been at the top of your game, using your abilities, attributes, and experience to succeed. The ensuing feeling of satisfaction, however, may seem incomplete if it cannot be shared with others. Consider the Decision-Making Formula to recognize the importance of avoiding inaction and isolation, two of the fundamentals of failure, or, in essence, visualize the importance of close relationships.

> If (natural abilities + attributes of success) + (observations/practices) > (fundamentals of failure) = correct decision-making.

Four of the fundamentals of failure—silence, human error, incompetence, and fear—can originate from outside yourself, though falsity originates from within. But even if you've escaped those five fundamentals of failure, you still might not attain a sense of satisfaction or contentment if you achieve success while alone, illustrating again that the presence of one fundamental of failure, in this instance two (isolation and inaction), can overwhelm your top abilities, attributes, and experiences.

No one knows precisely what has led Americans to withdraw from other people. In what has become a classic book, *Bowling Alone: The Collapse and Revival of American Community* (2000), Professor Robert Putnam chronicled a diminution in the number and quality of relationships among virtually every group. Putnam summarized some of the hollow conditions in America:

> We maintain a facade of formal affiliation, but we rarely show up. We have invented new ways of expressing our demands that demand less of us. We are less likely to turn out for collective deliberation.... We are less generous with our money and...with our time, and we are less likely to give strangers the benefit of the doubt. They, of course, return the favor.[189]

Putnam provides a comprehensive study of the decline of community in America but does not identify a specific reason why the decline has occurred. He writes: "Whatever one's detailed assessment of the reversal of the tide [of community] in the last two or three decades [prior to 2000], its very suddenness, thoroughness, and unexpectedness constitute an intriguing mystery."[190]

Putman summarized some of the sources of disconnection offered by commentators: lack of time, economics, two-career families, residential mobility, housing sprawl, technology, globalization, family disruption, larger welfare state, civil rights revolution, and cultural changes, beginning with the Vietnam War. But he could not identify a primary cause for isolation.[191]

Nonetheless, he saw the disconnection, the loss of "social capital," as a big problem for individuals and society. "It is, if I am right, a puzzle of some importance to the future of American democracy," presumably because a government functions better when more people communicate and contribute.[192]

Across a generation, in 2023, the US surgeon general, Vivek Murthy, found that loneliness is an epidemic and suggested that the four "keys to connection" are speaking on the phone, sharing a meal, meaningful conversations, and serving other people.[193]

Murthy's report concluded, "Loneliness is far more than just a bad feeling—it harms both individual and societal health. It is associated with a greater risk of cardiovascular disease, dementia, stroke, depression, anxiety, and premature death. The mortality impact of being socially disconnected is similar to that caused by smoking up to 15 cigarettes a day, and even greater than that associated with obesity and physical inactivity."[194]

But the surgeon general's report did not convincingly explain why "from 2003 to 2020, time spent alone increased, while time spent on in-person social engagement decreased."[195] The report suggested that at least twenty-eight "factors shape social connection," but did not identify a primary factor or significantly discuss any of them.[196]

In 2025, Professor Putnam, twenty-five years after *Bowling Alone*, found that withdrawal and loneliness remained entrenched in the populace. He and a coauthor focused on the "male malaise." They found, "Since 2010, suicide rates among young men have risen by a third—they are now higher than they are among middle-aged men. The share of college degrees going to men has fallen to 41 percent, lower than the women's share in 1970. One in 10 men aged 20 to 24 is effectively doing nothing—neither enrolled in school nor working. That's twice the rate in 1990."[197]

They cautioned not to blame overuse of social media, lack of education, or fewer job opportunities. Men and boys "are lost, in part because they are lonely: 25 percent of boys and men aged 15 to 34 told Gallup they had experienced loneliness 'a lot' on the previous day. One in seven young men reports that he has no close friends, up from 3 percent in 1990. Two thirds of men under the age of 30 think that 'no one cares if men are okay.'"

The crisis of withdrawal and loneliness is attached to the concept of deaths of despair, which originated to designate the feelings of hopelessness that produce deaths from suicide, alcohol abuse, and drug overdoses, "a form of ill-being akin to extreme unhappiness," according to researchers who produced the 2025 World Happiness Report.[198]

In the US, there were about forty-nine deaths of despair per one hundred thousand people, which was more than all of the fifty-nine countries, except for Slovenia and Guyana, that had available records that could be used for a survey.[199] In the countries with lower death rates, the average rate of death per one hundred thousand was about ten for women and thirty-seven for men.[200]

For society, especially in Europe and the US, the researchers believed that social distrust and unhappiness lead to political polarization.[201] "The fall in life satisfaction cannot be explained by economic growth, at least not by average national income, as GDP per capita has been on the rise in the US and Western Europe since the mid-2000s. Rather, it could be blamed on the feelings of financial insecurity and loneliness experienced by Americans and Europeans—two symptoms of a damaged social fabric."[202]

Similarly, in 2024, Professor Jonathan Haidt described increasing despair among children, beginning in the 2010s. Looking for the reasons behind children's detachment from society, he found that technology had "rewired" their thinking:

> The most intense period of this rewiring was 2010 to 2015, although the story…begins with the rise of fearful and overprotective parenting in the 1980s and continues through the COVID pandemic to the present day.[203] There's a second plotline here: the well-intentioned and disastrous shift toward overprotecting children and restricting their autonomy in the real world.[204] Now, as I write in 2023, there's a lot more research—experimental as well as correlational—showing that social media harms adolescents, especially girls going through puberty.[205]

Among children and adults in the US, as well as in many places throughout the world, researchers have identified what appears to be a decline in individuals' happiness, the essence of a good life. This is disappointing, as well as perplexing, because the modern world has produced efficiencies and opportunities through new methods of communication and transportation that enable more relationships than in the past.

THE CONDITIONS OF HAPPINESS: KNOWLEDGE, EXERCISE, AND CLOSE RELATIONSHIPS

Though many variables and circumstances contribute to happiness, three conditions form the deepest, strongest roots of it: knowledge, exercise, and close relationships. Fortunately, we know that simple modifications of behavior, though often challenging, can promote all three conditions. Usually, everything good begins with knowledge, the first condition.

Almost extinct today because of a decades-long behavioral initiative by the Carter Center in Georgia, the Guinea worm is a parasite that thrived in fetid ponds in Pakistan, India, and northern Africa. Villagers, after drinking from ponds, their only sources of water, would find that over the next year the parasites would grow inside their bodies into worms of two to three feet long. Then, over weeks or months, the worms, sometimes one but often several or a half-dozen, would force their way through the villagers' bodies and slowly ease their way through the skin.

The worms' crawling from the body caused excruciating pain and left villagers with debilitating deformities, often from amputations required when the worms exited from the lower extremities, especially the feet, though the worms exited from every part of the body. The worms, as they crawled slowly through the skin, could be coaxed to increase their pace by pouring water over the exit holes. The worms perceived they were in ponds, where they could lay their millions of larvae.

There is no vaccine to protect people from Guinea worms and no medicine to kill or expel the worms once they are inside the body. The only way to save people from the worms was to convince villagers to change their behavior. If their drinking water is from the ponds, the villagers should pour the water through a mesh filter before consuming it. When villagers were found to have contracted Guinea worm, local officials and workers from the Carter Center and other nongovernmental organizations would try to find the ponds that were the source and use chemicals to kill the parasites.

Where underground water existed, bore holes were drilled and the parasite-free water was extracted and consumed by the villagers. But some of them, until they learned how to change their behavior through education, would bypass the water from the bore holes because of its salty taste and drink the water from the ponds, which tasted better. Early on, because the parasites take a year to form into worms and eventually crawl outside the body, some villagers did not connect the pond water they drank a year ago to their current affliction. Through education, everyone now knows the danger of the Guinea worm. The number of Guinea worm cases has gone from 3.5 million in 1986 to thirteen in 2024.[206]

Guinea worm and the illnesses that it caused were eradicated primarily because of one behavior: education. Behavioral change, however, despite the benefits, can be a difficult emotional, mental, and social undertaking. In 2026, the US National Center for Health Statistics reported that, at birth, females in the US can expect to live 81.4 years and males 76.5 years (94 percent as long as females).[207] Men work in more dangerous jobs, such as logging, commercial fishing, roofing, and construction and engage in riskier behaviors (such as smoking), while they also appear to have chromosomes that lead to earlier death compared with women.

For a 2025 study, researchers examined the "life expectancy of 528 mammal and 648 bird species in zoos. Like humans, 72% of mammals exhibited a female life expectancy advantage, while 68%

of birds showed a male advantage, as expected from the harmful sex chromosomes as described by the heterogametic [different sex chromosomes] sex hypothesis."[208]

But remarkably, there is an easy way for all men and women, on average, to increase the number of years they will live: exercise. For a 2016 study, researchers tried to find whether people have inherited genes that help them live longer. In examining 1,354 people who ranged in age from 80 to 105 years old, they concluded: "We identified no major, singular contributor to healthy aging."[209] That means that almost no one has an innate advantage; living long depends on your behavior.

Aside from the chromosomal differences in men and women, people appear not to be genetically predisposed to living longer or, for example, dying sooner from lung or colon cancer, stroke, or type 2 diabetes. But their behavior and environmental risk factors—essentially how they treat their bodies and where they live—do increase the risk of acquiring these diseases. There are two exceptions. Because the long-living subjects did not suffer from Alzheimer's disease and coronary heart disease, the researchers concluded that genetic factors do increase the risk of those diseases. "On the other hand [these long-lived subjects] have a significantly lower genetic risk for Alzheimer disease...and coronary artery disease."[210]

Positive behaviors such as education, lifelong learning, and the reduction of risky activities, as well as an increase in regular exercise, will foster a stronger body and brain, as well as suppress diseases that are heritable (Alzheimer's and coronary artery disease).[211] With a foundation that preserves your body, you can continue the search for happiness by considering whether your own social conditions promote it. When life was harsher, "Classical and Enlightenment thinkers [late 1600s to early 1800s] defined happiness as the pursuit of virtue—as *being* good, rather than *feeling* good."[212]

Not always an aspiration, the quest for happiness "changed dramatically during the Enlightenment," when, through reasoning, Europeans began to understand the mechanics of the universe and deemphasized religious fatalism in the 1600s and 1700s. "On the one hand, it was now perfectly legitimate to seek happiness. On the other, not being happy, or at least not seeming to be, was a problem to be avoided," according to Professor Peter Stearns.

Daily living became easier, and people began to smile, possibly because better dentistry hid their embarrassment from tooth decay, according to one historian. In the 1800s, a new work ethic encouraged happiness. "The idea gained ground that heaven was a happy place marked by, among other things, blissful reunions with departed family members," a method to reduce fear or grief, according to Stearns. [213]

"Cultures that stress happiness likely…produce more happy people, but the link is complex and fragile," wrote Stearns, and too much focus on happiness promotes unrealistic expectations. "First, although the most obvious drawback of the emphasis on happiness involves the gaps with reality that can, paradoxically, create their own discontents, there's also the risk that people will fail to explore reasons for dissatisfaction because of pressure to exhibit good cheer…. Second, and at least as important, a culture saturated with happiness makes it difficult for people to deal with sadness, in themselves and others."[214]

In sum, despite all the good things that you can acquire or embody, including a state of virtue if that's possible or desirable, you likely will not be happy unless you have close, positive relationships with other people. A landmark study on human development and aging, the Grant Study, named for its first benefactor, and known formally as the Harvard Study of Adult Development, began in 1938 and continues today. Its subjects were male undergraduates at Harvard. The study is important for the depth of the information it has produced through questionnaires and personal interviews over the decades, including with the relatives of the students. (It is not publicly known whether any student remains alive.)

A parallel study was done with inner-city students from Boston, and the results were generally the same. The "Harvard sample lived on average ten years longer than the inner-city sample. But 25 of the 456 inner-city kids grew up, went to college, and graduated from college." Those twenty-five inner-city college graduates, on average, lived as long as the Harvard sample. The fourth director of the study, Robert Waldinger, concluded in 2023 that everyone with a college education in the mid-1900s would understand the harmful effects of smoking and would be less likely to take up the habit and live longer.[215]

The data from the study are available only periodically to researchers, and then only by visiting Harvard. One reason for restrictions is to ensure that the identity of the subjects remains confidential. For an article in the June 2009 edition of *The Atlantic*, "What Makes Us Happy," Joshua Wolf Shenk, the author, visited Harvard and, for a month, examined the data. Shenk, reading between the lines, concluded that one of the subjects became president, John F. Kennedy. Four of the subjects became candidates for the US Senate.

One troubling finding, however, was that by age fifty, almost one-third of them showed signs of mental illness.[216] Nonetheless, the study indicates that the following "protective factors" promote enrichment throughout the lifespan:

- Exercise.
- Weight control.

- Not smoking.
- Not abusing alcohol.
- Mental health.
- Education.
- Close and stable relationships.

This number of protective factors, seven, is not large. It is even smaller when noting that three of the protective factors (regarding weight, smoking, and alcohol) can be subsumed within mental health.

The number of protective factors then becomes only four: exercise, mental health, education, and close relationships. Using all seven protective factors, Shenk found that you need four of the seven factors to live a good life. "Even if they had been in adequate physical shape at 50, the men [in the study] who had three or fewer protective factors were three times as likely to be dead at 80 as those with four or more factors."

Both mental health and physical health are critical to happiness and longevity. Shenk found that "depression turned out to be a major drain on physical health: of the men who were diagnosed with depression by age 50, more than 70 percent had died or were chronically ill by 63. More broadly, pessimists seemed to suffer physically in comparison with optimists, perhaps because they're less likely to connect with others or care for themselves."[217]

Waldinger, the fourth director, summarized the importance of relationships in delaying death. "A core, and perhaps surprising, finding: Having good relationships—whether with partners, friends, family or others—is the 'strongest predictor' of living a long, healthy and happy life into old age, more so than health factors such as high blood pressure and cholesterol…. Social connections are really good for us…[and] loneliness kills."[218]

George Vaillant, another former director of the study, reached the same conclusion: "It is social aptitude, not intellectual brilliance or parental social class, that leads to successful aging."

Waldinger described the adverse physiological consequences stemming from the absence of a positive relationship. "The thinking about loneliness and social isolation is that if you don't have people to help you weather the inevitable stresses that come along, the body stays in a low-level fight-or-flight mode, with higher levels of circulating stress hormones and higher levels of inflammation, and we know that those things gradually wear away many different body systems."[219]

DOES MARRIAGE PROMOTE HAPPINESS?

The benefit of positive relationships raises an important nuts-and-bolts question—whether happiness requires marriage or a similar relationship. The answer appears to be *no*. The Grant study focused initially on its subjects' relationships with mothers in childhood, with fathers in childhood, and close relationships generally. "Warm" relationships in each category correlated with increased earnings throughout life. The "people who reported being most satisfied in close relationships at age 50 reported higher life satisfaction at age 80…[and] the value of close relationships at age 50 was found as a better predictor of life satisfaction than cholesterol level."[220]

As the participants in the Grant study aged, additional events in their lives could be considered, including marriage. Based on the study, one analysis described the effects of marriage on the subjects:

> The other important result that's come from the expanded study has to do with marriages—in particular, mental health and marriage. Those who

> reported satisfaction in marriage reported more stability in moods, even when suffering with physical pain. Those who were unhappy in marriage reported more emotional and physical pain.[221]

A good marriage is associated with longevity, but a bad marriage and the absence of close relationships are not. Is there a difference between a good marriage and a good relationship that does not include marriage? The answer appears to be *no*.

Writing in his 2011 book *Thinking, Fast and Slow*, Daniel Kahneman, a Princeton professor who in 2002 won the Nobel Prize in Economics (despite being a psychologist), cited a study "in which the same respondents were asked every year about their satisfaction with their life." Kahneman included a graph from the study that "shows the level of satisfaction reported by people around the time they got married."[222]

The results show that in the two years prior to marriage the respondents' satisfaction soared, and at the moment of marriage, their satisfaction was double what it had been four years earlier. But in the two years after marriage their satisfaction plummeted, to where it had been two years prior to marriage. In the fifth year after marriage, the respondents' satisfaction was lower than it had been four years prior to marriage.

Kahneman wrote, "The graph reliably evokes nervous laughter from audiences, and the nervousness is easy to understand: after all, people who decide to get married do so either because they expect it will make them happier or because they hope that making a tie permanent will maintain the present state of bliss."[223]

Kahneman summarized the studies he reviewed and concluded that people who are married or live with someone are not happier than people who are not married or do not live with someone. He explained:

> In the…studies, there was no overall difference in experienced well-being between women who live with a mate and women who did not. The details of how the two groups used their time explained the finding. Women who have a mate spend less time alone, but also much less time with friends. They spend more time making love, which is wonderful, but also more time doing housework, preparing food, and caring for children, all relatively unpopular activities. And of course, the large amount of time married women spend with their husband is much more pleasant for some than for others. Experienced well-being is on average unaffected by marriage, not because marriage makes no difference to happiness but because it changes some aspects of life for the better and others for the worse.[224]

Kahneman explained succinctly what the Grant study seems to have shown over decades: a good relationship is enriching, and a bad one is not.

In 2021, researchers, in describing the results from their two studies, reached the same conclusion, that the well-being of mates increases prior to marriage and decreases after marriage. They refuted or qualified "decades of research [that] have documented the apparent health benefits of marriage." In effect, they found that two well-adapted people who marry could be happy and that two well-adapted people who do not marry could be equally happy.

The traditional perception that marriage is more beneficial emotionally than not being married appears to be illusory. In their studies, the researchers found no connection between marriage and mental health:

- "Our first hypothesis was that individuals who transition to marriage would report increases in general health. This hypothesis was not supported."
- "Individuals who transition to marriage were expected to report increases in life satisfaction. This hypothesis was not supported."
- "Our hypothesis that individuals who transition to marriage would report less psychological distress over time was also not supported."
- "Our fourth hypothesis was that individuals who transition to marriage will report consuming less alcohol over time. This hypothesis was not supported. Alcohol use had been decreasing before marriage…but began increasing following marriage."[225]

Men and women view marriage differently, but their physical and mental health and general well-being are the same regardless of whether they are married.

The researchers found that "men reported an increase in life satisfaction right at the point of marriage while women reported a decrease at that point of transition. Similarly, women, but not men, experienced decreases in psychological distress before marriage and an increase following."

The researchers concluded, "No sustained improvements in mental and physical wellbeing were demonstrated across the marriage transition, and the gains that were observed were concentrated in the months leading up to marriage."[226]

In sum, happiness goes up and down in the year before and after marriage, but someone's happiness overall is not affected by marriage. Close relationships do include marriage, and people who marry and live long together might be happy. But the reason for their happiness is that they have a close relationship, not because it is formalized with marriage. Professor Kahneman described it this way: "Even newlyweds who are lucky enough to enjoy a state of happy preoccupation with their love will eventually return to earth, and their experienced well-being will again depend, as it does for the rest of us, on the environment and activities of the present moment."[227]

Shenk, the author of the *Atlantic* article on the Grant study, cited the importance of openness, and indicated that it should not be limited to close relationships. He described the bittersweet story of a man, one of the subjects, who did not realize his value to many other people and patients once he became a physician.

> What we do affects how we feel just as much as how we feel affects what we do. To illustrate his point, he [George Vaillant] told a story about one of his "prize" Grant Study men, a doctor and well-loved husband. "On his 70th birthday," Vaillant said, "when he retired from the faculty of medicine, his wife got hold of his patient list and secretly wrote to many of his longest-running patients, 'Would you write a letter of appreciation?' And back came 100 single-spaced, desperately loving letters—often with pictures attached. And she put them in a lovely presentation box covered with Thai silk and gave it to him." Eight years later, Vaillant interviewed the man, who proudly pulled the box down from

> his shelf. 'George, I don't know what you're going to make of this,' the man said, as he began to cry, 'but I've never read it.' "It's very hard," Vaillant said, "for most of us to tolerate being loved."

From what we know, it's not the search for virtue but rather a human connection that is the most important condition in living a good life and finding happiness.

"Warm connections are necessary—and if not found in a mother or father, they can come from siblings, uncles, friends, mentors. The men's relationships at age 47…predicted late-life adjustment better than any other variable, except [adaptive] defenses," according to Shenk.

This finding is consistent with the Decision-Making Formula. You might possess all the positive variables (abilities, attributes, and experiences), but if you don't avoid or defend against the seven fundamentals of failure—if you don't employ "adaptive defenses"—then you'll be less likely to attain enrichment or happiness.

Fortunately, positive relationships, along with your abilities, attributes, and experiences, will help to outweigh the fundamentals of failure. You should try to develop relationships as soon as possible; doing so will probably extend your life. The Grant study showed, according to Shenk, that "93 percent of the men who were thriving at age 65 had been close to a brother or sister when younger."

Shenk cited an interview of Vaillant in a 2008 newsletter to the subjects of the study. Vaillant was asked, "What have you learned from the Grant Study men?"

"That the only thing that really matters in life are your relationships to other people."

The 2025 World Happiness Report, by researchers at the University of Oxford, Gallup, and the UN, also stressed the importance of social interactions—and the finding is a life-or-death matter. The Happiness Report described the kinds of interactions that are most important:

- caring and sharing.
- living with others.
- supporting others.
- trusting others.
- giving to others.

The report provided one easily identifiable measure to evaluate your connections to other people: the number of times each week you share a meal with someone.

"Dining alone is strongly associated with substantial differences in subjective wellbeing for both men and women, young and old alike," the researchers found. [228] "In the United States, people who dine with others report more happiness and people who dine alone report more stress, pain, and sadness."[229]

Researchers asked respondents the number of times they had lunch or dinner with someone they knew in the last seven days. Of the ten regions in the world, people in the Latin America and Caribbean region shared the most meals per week, nine. People in the South Asia region shared the fewest, four, and East Asia was next lowest, at just under six, indicating more people in South Korea and Japan living alone.

The average number of shared meals in the North America, Australia and New Zealand, and Western European regions was just over eight. The country with the highest number of shared meals each week was Senegal, at 11.8, followed by Gambia, Malaysia, and Paraguay, with 11 shared meals each week.[230]

Most interactions contribute to the attainment of happiness. "Relationships based on affection, close communication, repeated contact, and mutual support are a source of family satisfaction and, in turn, life satisfaction as a whole," according to the Happiness Report.[231] Both "extroverts and introverts derive happiness from social interactions, but for different reasons."[232]

Remember that party, play, concert, lecture, race, barbeque, or bowling game you thought about attending but, instead, decided to stay home? That was probably a mistake. The researchers found, "People are not very accurate in forecasting how they will feel after engaging in social activities, leading them to miss out on opportunities to connect."[233]

HOW MUCH MONEY DO YOU NEED TO BE HAPPY?

In interviews over the years, including for *Men's Journal* in 2008 when he was seventy-five, Willie Nelson, the popular singer, would be asked what he had learned about women. "What one thing should every man know about women?" the interviewer asked.

"Well, Ray Price [another singer] told me that the only thing he'd learned about women is that money makes them horny. I couldn't argue with that."[234]

Willie Nelson's whimsical response about his apparently amorous experiences is well supported by more scientific studies. In 2012, researchers reported, "Our results reject the popular idea individuals seek money in their mates per se; instead, they seem to seek mates who have earned their money." Women found men less desirable when they had inherited or embezzled their money. "Earning his money may denote deeper, more important underlying qualities. Although men preferred women who earned their money over other sources, this effect was much less pronounced than it was in women."[235]

One conclusion is that the Beatles song "[Money] Can't Buy Me Love" is probably less realistic than ABBA's song "Money, Money, Money," in which one of the female vocalists sings about her desire to find a wealthy man. Though we might find it difficult to acknowledge, if happiness depends on relationships, and if some relationships depend on money, then money contributes to happiness.

Most people would agree that money provides increased stability and security. Writing in 2019, a psychology professor, David Ludden, summarized the characteristics that are attractive to men and women. "One of the most robust findings in evolutionary psychology is the observation that men and women differ in the characteristics they prefer in potential mates. In study after study, in country after country, psychologists consistently find that men strongly prefer looks over resources, whereas women value resources over looks."[236]

In 2016, researchers reached the same conclusion after conducting studies into the effects of money on heterosexual relationships of college students in China. According to the researchers, "The findings from our two experiments reveal that the feeling of having relatively more or less money could cause differences in mating strategies.... From the perspective of evolution, these...psychological mechanisms still play important roles in human mating. The practical implication of our findings is to remind people to pay attention to the potential changes brought about by changes in the amount of money they possess."[237]

Citing evolution, Professor Ludden found that the reason for the different preferences is that "fertile women who will bear high-quality offspring" are valued for the "characteristics of feminine beauty—such as low waist-to-hip ratio, clear skin, and lustrous hair—[which]

are all signs of good health, so it's only natural that men would find these attractive."[238]

Money is an element of happiness, but how much money must one possess to be happy? In the 2025 Happiness Report, aside from the social interactions that contribute to happiness, a nation's gross domestic product per capita is a primary measure of happiness. The countries atop the happiness rating were (1–5) Finland, Denmark, Iceland, Sweden, and the Netherlands, all with financial resources to provide healthy, long lives for the people living there. The lowest rated countries on the happiness scale (143–147) were Zimbabwe, Malawi, Lebanon, Sierra Leone, and Afghanistan, some of the poorest countries. The US was rated number twenty-four in happiness.[239]

As additional evidence that money contributes to happiness, recall the five countries where people ate meals together most frequently (an indicator of happiness), Senegal, Gambia, Malaysia, and Paraguay. They were ranked 107, 117, 64, and 54, respectively, in happiness, seemingly in line with their financial resources.

When two eminent scholars, one of whom was Professor Kahneman, the Nobel Prize winner who studied the value of marriage, suggested in 2010 that between $60,000 and $90,000 yearly in household income, in the US, would be sufficient, on the money element, to produce happiness, families and individuals derived hope that they could be as happy as rich people. The other scholar was Angus Deaton, another Princeton professor, who would win the Nobel Prize in Economics in 2015.

Seeming to support the Beatles (money can't buy you love), Kahneman and Deaton appeared also to have proven the proposition that money can't buy you happiness. They found, "Emotional well-being also rises with…income, but there is no further progress beyond an annual income of ~$75,000. Low income exacerbates the emotional pain associated with such misfortunes as divorce, ill health, and being alone. We conclude that high income buys life satisfaction but not happiness, and that low income is associated both with low life evaluation and low emotional well-being."[240]

But, alas, contrary to the findings of the Nobel Prize winners, more money does produce more happiness. In 2021, Kahneman's and Deaton's conclusion, that income greater than $75,000 does not lead to much greater happiness, was challenged by another scholar, Matthew Killingsworth. He found "that happiness rose steadily with income well beyond $75,000, without evidence of a plateau."[241] In other words, more money means more happiness.

Killingsworth was correct. In what is known as an adversarial collaboration, Kahneman and Killingsworth agreed to reexamine together the available data and, in 2023, along with a facilitator, Professor Barbara Mellers, coauthored an article on the findings of their new study. Kahneman and Deaton, the Nobel Prize winners, had largely been wrong.[242]

In the new study, Killingsworth and Kahneman, along with Mellers, found "that, on average, larger incomes are associated with ever-increasing levels of happiness...[but] an unhappy cohort in each income group shows a sharp rise in happiness up to $100,000 annually and then plateaus."[243]

Kahneman and Deaton, in 2010, had applied this latter finding, that there is a plateau of happiness, to every household that earns about $75,000. But the new study showed that this plateau applies only to people who are generally unhappy.

Killingsworth explained, "In the simplest terms, this suggests that for most people larger incomes are associated with greater happiness. The exception is people who are financially well-off but unhappy. For instance, if you're rich and miserable, more money won't help. For everyone else, more money was associated with higher happiness to somewhat varying degrees."[244]

Mellers, the facilitator in the study, noted that the findings do not show that money, alone, produces happiness. "The function differs for people with different levels of emotional well-being. Specifically, for the least happy group, happiness rises with income until $100,000, then shows no further increase as income grows. For those in the middle range of emotional well-being, happiness increases linearly with income, and for the happiest group the association actually accelerates above $100,000."[245]

In sum, there is an unhappy minority of people, 15 to 20 percent, who will become less unhappy when earning more money, but only up to $100,000, and no amount of money beyond that will lead to happiness for them. "The suffering of the unhappy group diminishes as income increases up to 100k but very little beyond that. This income threshold may represent the point beyond which the miseries that remain are not alleviated by high income. Heartbreak, bereavement, and clinical depression may be examples of such miseries," according to Killingsworth, Kahneman, and Mellers.[246]

In contrast, they found, "In the happier majority, happiness continues to rise with income even in the high range of incomes."[247]

Though a sufficient amount of money is necessary to retain or increase your happiness, the amount will vary based on the cost of living in your region. In 2022, a middle-income household (of three persons), depending on location in the US, earned from $56,600 to $169,800, and perhaps you could consider an amount in that range to be sufficient.[248]

But small incremental increases in money will not lead to big jumps in happiness. Only a doubling of money, according to one report, from $50,000 to $100,00, for example, will accelerate a big jump in happiness.[249] Generally someone who invests her money in stocks and bonds must wait 7.1 years and 9.9 years, respectively, before the stocks and bonds double in value.[250] This means that you will likely need to formulate a reliable plan, facilitated by sound decision-making, to achieve your goals, including happiness, which does not occur naturally or overnight.

THE TEN ELEMENTS OF HAPPINESS

We need not despair because money, though necessary, is only one element of happiness. From studies and observations, you may find that ten primary elements contribute to happiness, though your experience might lead to other elements as well. If one of the elements has too little substance, such as not enough money, you can compensate for it with other elements that have plenty of substance, such as health, education, and relationships.

Every person will weigh and value the elements differently, but, overall, you should possess a sufficient number of them, at a sufficiently high level, to attain happiness. The ten elements of happiness are as follows:

1. Health.
2. Autonomy.
3. Relationships.
4. Education.
5. Trust.
6. Humility.
7. Peacefulness.
8. Philanthropy.
9. Money.
10. Optimism.

The final element, optimism, is the connection between the present and future. Optimism here does not concern predictions in the way that corporate executives expect higher earnings or managers project hopefulness to obscure bad news. Instead, optimism arises from the knowledge that other people understand what you feel, that through communication, contact, and sharing, you will enrich each other. Whether young or old, optimism means that, as you age, you will know that someone will support or encourage you in many endeavors and be close to you at the end.

Key Points

- Close relationships are to happiness as water is to life.
- Marriage does not increase or decrease happiness.
- Money does increase happiness.
- You can attain the ten elements of happiness, but action is required.
- Autonomy and sharing are indispensable.

CHAPTER 8

LIVING, AND DYING AFTER A MEANINGFUL LIFE

(WHEN YOU HAVE NO MORE CONTROL)

In this final chapter, by considering the decisions people make when death is near, you can decide what you'd like to accomplish before then and what discussions you'd like to have with the people who are most important to you. Though perhaps once believing that acceptance and quietude accompany the latter moments of life, you'll be reminded that inaction is a fundamental of failure, at any age. To the moment when you have no further capacity, when your abilities have dissipated or perished, you can make decisions that positively affect your future, however long it might be. To help you make decisions at the end for other people, as well as for yourself, consider first an earlier transition, from childhood to adulthood, and a promising seventeen-year-old college student in New York City.

In 1979, the student, Grace Gold, was struck in the head and killed by a piece of masonry that had dislodged from a tall building.

As a result, the city, in 1980, enacted a law requiring the inspections of building facades and the creation of scaffolding sheds, which shield pedestrians below when inspections and repairs of buildings occur. Today, the metal pipes and beams supporting the sheds sprout from steel platforms on the sidewalks, requiring pedestrians to walk in zigzag fashion throughout the city. For a more direct pathway, many pedestrians walk in the streets instead.

By 2024, the city had more than 8,500 sheds, considered by almost everyone to be eyesores, and 1,000 of the sheds had stood for more than three years, with some dating to 2011. Building owners find it cheaper to leave the sheds in place, thereby complying with city regulations, than to fulfill the purpose of the sheds, to protect people below during temporary inspections and repairs of buildings. If placed in a line, the sheds would extend from New York City to Montreal, Canada, 372 miles, a six-hour drive by automobile. Creating a shroud of darkness in hidden alcoves, the sheds are used as encampments by homeless people and drug dealers.[251]

Officials do not know how many injuries have been avoided or lives saved by the sheds over the past forty-six years. An investigation by the *New York Times* found that pedestrian deaths occurred from falling debris during building construction in the late nineteenth and early twentieth centuries, but the investigation did not identify any deaths, other than the college student in 1979, from debris that fell from completed buildings because "there aren't many instances involving random pieces of dislodged masonry."[252]

The shed situation introduces the question of whether there is anything more important than human life. Do decades of inconvenience and lost time created by the sheds outweigh the value of one human life saved? How should the demoralizing effect and decrease in quality of life caused by the ugly sheds be valued? Currently, the construction of the sheds, as well as the commercial interests lobbying for and against them, is a billion-dollar business, with store owners who want unobstructed passageways versus shed builders.[253]

The abolition of the sheds, which would mean the reallocation of at least a billion dollars, might help save many lives. As the shed situation illustrates, though, the question of whether there is anything more important than life is deceptively difficult to answer. Almost everyone is surprised to learn that he or she believes an innocent person, for instance, should sometimes be allowed to die or, more disturbingly, intentionally killed if necessary to benefit society. How can that be?

Consider the case of an automobile driver operating a car (legally in all respects). The driver, accompanied by three passengers, is driving downward on a steep mountain road. The driver turns around a switchback and sees a small, helpless child in the middle of the narrow road. Someone else is responsible for the child's presence in the road, but that is irrelevant because the driver's decision does not depend on past events, only the present. The driver must select one of only two options that are available: knowingly drive over and kill the child or drive off the road and into a canyon five-thousand feet below and kill himself and the other three passengers in the car. Almost everyone will search for a third alternative, not recognizing that sometimes there is nothing you can do to avoid tragedy.

In contemplating whether to drive over the child or off the cliff, some might argue that neither the driver nor anyone else—to encourage nonviolence—should ever intentionally kill an innocent person, such as the child. Like police officers and soldiers, the argument goes, we have a greater obligation to society, and in a few circumstances, we must sacrifice our lives because adherence to nonviolence now will save a greater number of lives in the future, perhaps through more peaceful people starting fewer wars. However, the crisis on the mountain makes us less certain of the nonviolence argument (do not kill an innocent person). That's because the driver, in one of only two possible actions (based on the driver's decision), must either kill the child or the four people in the car by driving off the cliff.

THE FIREFIGHTER'S DILEMMA

This leads to another problem that is more difficult to resolve. Should society authorize killing an innocent person to save property or something inanimate? Imagine there is a fire at one of the world's most important museums. Firefighters are responding and, if not delayed, will arrive in time to save all the treasures in the museum. If they are delayed, the fire will ignite a gas tank, and all the treasures will be destroyed.

Despite the sirens and flashing lights on the fire trucks, an elderly person who cannot see the lights or hear the sirens enters a crosswalk at an intersection. The firefighter driving the lead truck has two choices. First, the firefighter could decrease the speed of the truck and avoid killing the elderly person, in which event all the treasures would be destroyed. The other alternative is to maintain speed and run over and kill the elderly person and arrive in time to save the treasures. Would this decision be more complicated if the fire truck driver knew that the elderly person had only one week to live? Would the decision be more difficult if you knew that driving over the elderly person would allow the firefighters to arrive in time to save the formula for the cure for cancer?

As you have observed, life-or-death decision-making is not hypothetical. Assume that the firefighters are rushing to the US Centers for Disease Control, in Atlanta, Georgia, to try to prevent one of two live smallpox samples in the world from escaping and killing a large number of people. (The Vector Laboratory in Siberia, Russia, is the other location where live smallpox virus is stored.) Would you agree now that the firefighters should run over the elderly person to prevent the release of the smallpox?

ALIVE, BUT AT WHAT COST?

In the 1884 English case, *Her Majesty the Queen v. Tom Dudley and Edwin Stephens*, the accused men, along with another seaman, Edmund Brooks, and a seventeen-year-old cabin boy, Richard Parker, tried to sail a fifty-two-foot yacht, the *Mignonette*, from England to Australia. Precarious given the best large ship in the late 1800s, the fifteen-thousand-mile-long voyage was more likely to be fatal for the sailors on such a small boat.

The yacht's owner hired the four sailors to shepherd the yacht to Australia. Almost predictably, over 1,500 miles northwest of the Cape of Good Hope (South Africa), the *Mignonette*, on an apparently quiet night, was struck by a giant rogue wave and sank within five minutes. The four crew members jumped hastily into their lifeboat, which was about four yards long.

They were able to take with them two tins of turnips. Over the next twenty days, they ate the turnips and one turtle that they had caught, and they drank a few droplets of rainwater. By day twenty, all of them were near death from starvation and dehydration, especially the cabin boy, Parker, who had foolishly drunk salty seawater. "Human kidneys can only make urine that is less salty than salt water. Therefore, to get rid of all the excess salt taken in by drinking seawater, you have to urinate more water than you drank. Eventually, you die of dehydration even as you become thirstier," according to the National Oceanic and Atmospheric Administration.[254]

Dudley and Stephens, with families, decided that Parker, who was nearest death and unable to move, should be sacrificed so the other three castaways would have a chance to live. They enlisted Brooks, too, but he claimed later to have refused to join the conspiracy to kill Parker. Dudley and Stephens prayed over Parker before Dudley, the captain of the yacht, knifed Parker in the neck.

Brooks, despite claiming not to be a conspirator, and Dudley and Stephens consumed Parker's corpse and drank his blood. A few days later, a total of twenty-four days after the sinking of the *Mignonette*, a passing ship rescued the three surviving sailors.

Back in England and thinking they had acted according to the laws of nature, Dudley and Stephens, as well as Brooks, explained to authorities what had happened, including the details surrounding the killing of Parker. Despite public sentiment on their side, Dudley and Stephens were charged with murder, found guilty, and sentenced to death. But after six months in prison, they were pardoned by the Crown.

A defense of necessity—innocent people may be killed if necessary to ensure a greater good—is recognized in American law and outlined in the Model Penal Code, which was created by legal scholars and published in 1962. The principle from the code is utilitarian and applies to any situation when someone in an emergency must decide which of two evils to select, as the code describes the problem. That is, a killer should not be guilty if his killing of an innocent person (infant on a mountain, elderly pedestrian, or cabin boy) was less costly to society when compared with committing an alternative evil act, such as driving four people off a cliff.[255]

A similar decision for you might be closer than you imagine. Adult children must often decide whether to use their own money, time, and energy to provide care for their parents or send them to a nursing home. More expensive than a nursing facility, extensive in-home care for an elderly person can cost over $200,000 a year.[256] While some states provide support for residents who cannot afford to pay for nursing care, the adult children, regardless, face a heartbreaking choice: provide modest care at their parents' home and, thus, deplete their own resources or send their parents to nursing facilities, where their parents are more likely to die sooner than if they had remained in their own homes.

For a 2010 paper, researchers considered "1,817 nursing home residents who died between 1992 and 2006." The paper showed that 53 percent of the people who enter nursing homes die within six months, at an average age of 83.3 years old.

The median length of stay prior to death was five months. The average length of stay was 13.7 months, which accounted for a few residents who lived in nursing homes for years.[257]

Some nursing homes feel like sterile, cavernous crypts for a reason. The study showed that the median stay in nursing homes is three months for men and eight months for women. The median stay of residents in the top quartile of net worth (greater than $150,000) was three months, while the median stay for residents in the bottom quartile was nine months (under $3,000), presumably because the higher net-worth residents were able to afford care and remain in their own homes longer before entering a nursing facility.[258]

This appears to answer the question of whether elderly people live longer in their homes or nursing facilities. According to a 2021 study, "It is now well known that life expectancy declines when someone is admitted to a NH [nursing home].... In this paper, we presented evidence that the life expectancy decline is large, amounting to 45 months."[259]

Another question is whether people who enter nursing homes die sooner because they are sicker than the people who die at home.

The answer appears to be *no*. The study accounted for health conditions and found that an elderly person would live longer by not entering a nursing home:

> [E]ven controlling for many factors that determine a person's health state, life expectancy would still be reduced by 41 months from what it otherwise would have been if residing outside a NH. Surprisingly, the skilled nursing that is supposed to take place, and justify the very existence of NHs, had a worse impact than unskilled family care, or even no care at all.[260]

This study focused on nursing home residents with dementia, one of the leading causes of death. "We confirmed that people with serious dementia were more likely to reside in NHs, and they were more likely to have fewer years of life expectancy wherever they resided. However, they would have had 14 more months of life expectancy if they had not lived in NHs."[261]

The study explained that staffing levels help to determine mortality rates. "NH effectiveness in preserving life expectancy would be improved if both the quantity and quality of skilled nursing care were enhanced."[262]

Adult children might not have adequate money, time, or energy to care for their parents and find it necessary to move them to nursing homes. In a sense, then, their elderly parents are dying early for the benefit of their adult children. This teaches us not to be quick to judge the driver on the mountain who drives over the child or the firefighter on the way to the smallpox storage facility who drives over the elderly person. It might be that in their flimsy lifeboat, Dudley and Stephens, with their knife in hand and quest to live, are not very different from everyone else.

YOUR FINAL DECISION

Our work will end now by considering the final decision that any person could make. Recall Professor Daniel Kahneman, the 2002 Nobel Prize winner who measured the value of marriage and the amount of money necessary to achieve happiness. In March 2023, Kahneman and another researcher, Matthew Killingsworth found that unhappy people, about 15 to 20 percent of the population, can decrease their unhappiness by earning up to $100,000, but more money than that will not lead to an additional decrease in unhappiness for them. For everyone else, more money contributes to more happiness.[263]

A year later, in March 2024, Kahneman, born in 1934, was visiting Paris with his partner, Barbara Tversky. Kahneman's second wife, of forty years, had died in 2018. Tversky's husband, who had been Kahneman's close friend and collaborator, had died of cancer in 1996, at age fifty-nine. With Barbara Tversky, along with his children from an earlier first marriage, Kahneman's time in Paris, where he had grown up, was meaningful, though bittersweet. Several days later, Kahneman, still physically and mentally capable at ninety years old, traveled to Switzerland, which authorizes assisted dying for any competent person, whether in good or poor health.

Switzerland permits people who want to die to swallow lethal drugs or ingest gas inside a capsule. Canada allows physician-assisted dying and does not require a terminal illness, but it does require that the person who wishes to die "have a grievous and irremediable medical condition." Canada allows the person to swallow a fatal drug or receive from a medical practitioner a fatal injection. In the eleven US states (and the District of Columbia) that permit assisted dying, all of which require a terminal illness, people swallow lethal drugs.[264]

In Switzerland, the person who wishes to die in the capsule will climb inside, lie down, and close the hatch. The person must answer prerecorded questions and then press a button to flood the capsule with nitrogen, which lowers the level of oxygen from 21 to 1 percent. The person is likely to "feel disoriented or euphoric," according to the capsule's inventor.

"The whole thing takes about 30 seconds. Death takes place through hypoxia and hypocapnia, oxygen and carbon dioxide deprivation, respectively. There is no panic, no choking," according to the inventor.[265]

On March 27, 2024, Kahneman ended his life in Switzerland, according to his plan, though the method he used is not publicly known. Kahneman, especially because of his Nobel Prize and popular 2011 book, *Thinking, Fast and Slow*, was considered to be one of the preeminent experts on decision-making. What could lead a competent and physically able person, possibly one of the most analytical people in history, to choose death over life?

On March 19, 2024, just over a week before Kahneman died, two philosophy professors emailed Kahneman to ask him to agree to be interviewed on their podcast, *Lives Well Lived*. Kahneman, not yet in France, wrote back and included part of a letter that he would send to a few friends shortly before his appointed time in Switzerland: "I have believed since I was a teenager that the miseries and indignities of the last years of life are superfluous, and I am acting on that belief. I am still active, enjoying many things in life (except the daily news) and will die a happy man. But my kidneys are on their last legs, the frequency of mental lapses is increasing, and I am 90 years old. It is time to go."

In an April 2025 essay, more than a year after Kahneman's death, the professors, Katarzyna de Lazari-Radek, of the University of Lodz, in Poland, and Peter Singer, of Princeton, wrote of Kahneman: "But despite his advanced age, he was still capable of research and writing and could still enlighten audiences on how to make better decisions. Apart from his intellectual gifts, he was healthy enough to participate in friendship and family life. Why did none of this give him sufficient reason to continue to live?"[266]

The professors cited the interview they did with Kahneman. "The answer, we believe, can be found toward the end of the interview.... He surprised us by denying that his work had any objective significance."

Kahneman had said, "Other people happen to respect it and say that this is for the benefit of humanity. I just like to get up in the morning because I like the work. I feel I've lived my life well, but it's a feeling. I'm just reasonably happy with what I've done. I would say if there is an objective point of view, then I'm totally irrelevant to it. If you look at the universe and the complexity of the universe, what I do with my day cannot be relevant."

Professors Lazari-Radek and Singer disagreed with Kahneman's decision but concluded that "you are the best judge of what is good for you. This is especially clear in the case of people who are at an age at which they cannot hope for improvement in their quality of life."[267]

That is an obvious point because, at any age, everyone's decline can lead to loss of hope. Rather, how should someone decide that the loss of hope is so grave that he or she should die? The state of Oregon permits physicians to prescribe drugs that will induce death, but the person who wants to die is responsible for ingesting the drugs. In 2024, 607 people in Oregon received prescriptions for the lethal drugs, and 376 died after taking them. (Presumably, the others had a change of heart.) The most common terminal illnesses of the deceased people in Oregon were cancer (57 percent), neurological disease (15 percent), and heart disease (11 percent).[268]

As professors Lazari-Radek and Singer concluded, people lose hope. Oregon's study found, "Most patients died at home (83%), and most were enrolled in hospice care (92%).... As in previous years, the three most frequently reported end-of-life concerns were loss of autonomy (89%), decreasing ability to participate in activities that made life enjoyable (88%), and loss of dignity (64%)."[269]

Lazari-Radek and Singer concluded, "One lesson to learn from [Kahneman's] death is that if we are to live well to the end, we need to be able to freely discuss when a life is complete, without shame or taboo. Such a discussion may help people to know what they really want. We may regret their decisions, but we should respect their choices and allow them to end their lives with dignity."[270]

A reporter for the *Wall Street Journal*, Jason Zweig, had helped Kahneman conduct research for Kahneman's book, *Thinking, Fast and Slow*. Zweig accepted Kahneman's decision but questioned the reasoning behind it. "I never got to say goodbye to Danny and don't fully understand why he felt he had to go. His death raises profound questions: How did the world's leading authority on decision-making make the ultimate decision? How closely did he follow his own precepts on how to make good choices? How does his decision fit into the growing debate over the downsides of extreme longevity? How much control do we, and should we, have over our own death?"[271]

Zweig quoted from the letter that Kahneman sent to his friends shortly before his death.

> This is a goodbye letter I am sending friends to tell them that I am on my way to Switzerland, where

> my life will end on March 27.... Not surprisingly, some of those who love me would have preferred for me to wait until it is obvious that my life is not worth extending. But I made my decision precisely because I wanted to avoid that state, so it had to appear premature. I am grateful to the few with whom I shared early, who all reluctantly came round to support me. I discovered after making the decision that I am not afraid of not existing, and that I think of death as going to sleep and not waking up.... The last period has truly not been hard, except for witnessing the pain I caused others. So if you were inclined to be sorry for me, don't be.

These circumstances, a preeminent decision-maker choosing to die, allow a final application of the Decision-Making Formula. The formula appears to point to an incorrect decision to die because the positive variables in Kahneman's life appear to outweigh the negative variables, the seven fundamentals of failure. Recall the formula for one last time:

> If (natural abilities + attributes of success) + (observations/practices) > (fundamentals of failure) = correct decision-making.

Kahneman, though he thought his intellect might be slipping, appeared to retain a significant portion of his abilities (math, verbal, and perceptual), as evidenced by his reasoning in the final letter he wrote to his friends and his clarity on Lazari-Radek's and Singer's podcast, as well as his traveling to and through France and Switzerland. He appeared to embody the attributes of success (humility, empathy, fairness, and trust). Though his empathy might be questioned, given that his pending death caused grief in others, it would be difficult to conclude that their feelings should dictate his action or inaction.

He apparently continued his research until the end ("I just like to get up in the morning because I like the work"), thus adding to the remaining positive variables in his life (observations and practices). Kahneman had a partner and adult children and many friends and colleagues, a condition that satisfies the primary element of happiness (close relationships). Thus, it can be difficult to see how all these good things could be outweighed by one or more of the seven fundamentals of failure (silence, human error, incompetence, isolation, inaction, fear, and falsity).

However, his decision to die might have been correct because, unusual as it seems, death could be filed under the positive variables, not under the seven fundamentals of failure. In other words, when is death preferable to life? In his book, *Thinking, Fast and Slow*, Kahneman reported seeing an opera, Verdi's *La Traviata*, and described Violetta's young lover as he tries to reach her before she dies. "He does, of course [reach her], some marvelous love duets are sung, and after 10 minutes of glorious music Violetta dies."

Kahneman wrote, "On my way home from the opera, I wondered: Why do we care so much about those last 10 minutes? I quickly realized I did not care at all about the length of Violetta's life. If I had been told that she died at age 27, not age 28 as I believed, the news that she had missed a year of happy life would not have affected me at all, but the possibility of missing the last 10 minutes mattered a great deal."[272]

Kahneman explained that he had advised a colleague who, with other researchers, conducted a study on how people perceive the value of a happy life. The researchers posed to the subjects, college students, the question of what it would be like to add five "slightly happy years" to what had been, to this point, a "very happy" life. This, according to Kahneman, "caused a substantial drop in evaluations of the total happiness of that life."[273]

The subjects in the study wanted to die while very happy, and, for them, being only slightly happy over five additional years was not appealing. Kahneman was surprised at the results but then found that he understood the subjects' reasoning. "In spite of my long experience with judgment errors, I did not believe that reasonable people could say that adding 5 slightly happy years to a life would make it substantially worse. I was wrong. The intuition that the disappointing extra 5 years made the whole life worse was overwhelming."[274]

Kahneman had come to believe that a very happy final ten minutes of life were more valuable to him than five slightly happy years on top of those very happy final ten minutes. Recall from Oregon's study why terminally ill people choose to die—their loss of autonomy and decreasing ability to perform activities that were previously enjoyable. Kahneman chose complete autonomy in the last ten minutes of his life rather than risking that his autonomy would be diminished in the final five years. For many people, death is the ultimate fundamental of failure, thus making living, in whatever condition, the highest value. But for Professor Kahneman, living, at least at age ninety, was no longer the top value. Autonomy—the ability to decide whether to live or die according to his conscience—was the preeminent value.

Probably expressing the sentiment of almost everyone at one time or another, Kahneman wrote that given "the complexity of the universe, what I do with my day cannot be relevant." This feeling of smallness that each person feels brings you back to the first recommendation of this book: to have close relationships throughout life, and especially at the end of it. Emphasizing this, Professor Kahneman's final words to his friends were: "Thank you for helping make my life a good one."[275]

If you've learned from this book to live and die according to your conscience while accompanied by your friends, your remaining decisions, even in emergencies, will seem less distressing. Some decisions are inevitable, and some will be heartbreaking. But you know now what to expect and how to prepare. A physician, Shoshana Ungerleider, found that people nearing the very end of their lives express five regrets, all of which you can remedy through planning and prioritization long before that moment:

- I didn't spend enough time with the people I love.
- I worked too much and missed out on life.
- I let fear control my decisions and didn't take risks.
- I wish I'd been braver in the face of uncertainty or opportunity.
- I focused too much on the future and lost touch with the present.

Ungerleider recommends constantly asking yourself about two important matters so that you do not regret what happened in the past.

"How do I want to spend my time?"

"What matters most to me in my life?'[276]

Consider how you would feel if death were near, in the final moments when you can still speak. Another physician, oncologist Siddhartha Mukherjee, wrote, "Every person that I've met in this moment of transition wanted to make four offerings":

- I want to tell you that I love you.
- I want to tell you that I forgive you.
- Would you tell me that you love me?

- Would you give me your forgiveness?

Many dying people find they are too late "to show their appreciation for others or right their interpersonal wrongs," leading to Mukherjee's conclusion that you should incorporate love and forgiveness into daily activities.[277]

It is, indeed, time to get out of the chair, as Martha Shaw, then living in a shelter, concluded before she used her last dollars, paper currency, to pay for a modest new house with concrete supports to protect her against the next flood. In our getting to work, as Mukherjee found, and according to Richard Cowden, a psychologist, forgiveness includes responsibility, remorse, reorientation, and renewal.

First, accept and express that you've wronged another person. Second, after taking responsibility, accept that shame, guilt, and remorse may cloud your life temporarily. Third, if possible, try to right the wrong done to the other person. If that's not possible, express in some way what you would have done if given the opportunity. Fourth, try to "realize that everyone makes mistakes and that you are not beyond repair." When you cannot correct your mistakes, try to free yourself from any guilt that you feel.[278]

Robert Waldinger, one of the directors of the Grant study, showed how each of us has the capacity to find happiness. "There were two big items over 85 years: one is taking care of our health. The part that surprised us was that the people who were happiest, who stayed healthiest as they grew old, and who lived the longest were the people who had the warmest connections with other people.... It stands to reason that you'd be happier if you had good relationships—those two things go together—but how could good relationships predict that you'd be less likely to get coronary artery disease or type 2 diabetes or arthritis?"[279]

This insight about what factors increase longevity is valuable but should not be the final word on how to have a good life. You've found that the Decision-Making Formula can be applied to the smallest and largest problems to arrive at a correct decision. Through Professor Kahneman, who possessed all the positive variables and was presumably happy, you've seen that something more, autonomy for him, must be present if you are to experience peace of mind, if that's the best expression for not worrying.

Professor Gary Saul Morson, in a 2025 essay, tried to make sense of this feeling by thinking about the novels of Leo Tolstoy, the Russian author. In *Anna Karenina*, one of Tolstoy's books, the character Konstantin Levin "experiences this despair. Like Tolstoy, he was happily married and enjoyed running his prosperous estate. Yet he was nevertheless unaccountably 'stricken with horror' at life 'without any knowledge of whence, and why and how and what it was.'"[280]

Morson wrote that Levin, "having accepted the scientific worldview in place of religious faith, he turned to it for answers, only to realize it couldn't address questions of meaning."

Many people, outwardly successful and happy, may have questions they try to avoid for fear of not having the capacity to answer. "Levin also wondered why, when he didn't focus on the questions that drove him to despair but simply lived, 'it seemed as though he knew both what he was and why he was living, for he acted resolutely.' He took care of his family, interested himself in the welfare of his peasant employees, and managed his sister's property, not because of some 'general principles' but because these actions were 'incontestably necessary.' It was…impossible not to care for those dependent on him."

Like many people, Levin could not satisfy his search for meaning. "Levin's problem is that he assumes, as intellectuals often do, that truth is a matter of theory that one applies to particular circumstances. That is how mathematics works, but questions of meaning and ethics are different. They require unformalizable wisdom, which arises from sensitive reflection about specific cases, and demand we trust our experience with particulars.... Like Tolstoy, Levin told himself he must answer his questions or die: 'Without knowing what I am and why I am here, life's impossible.'"

Professor Morson concluded, "One directly senses the meaning of existence by living rightly. It isn't a proposition or philosophy that can be taught. All one can do is indicate the sort of thing meaning is by showing how someone found it."[281]

That, too, is what we've tried to do, to learn to make sense of and find meaning in our most important decisions. You've observed how to identify the elements of happiness, and you may continue to wonder whether what you have or feel is all there is. In response to uncertainty, you know the importance of adapting to the present conditions. Along the way, find the goodness in others, know that only the present is guaranteed, and enjoy relationships. At every moment, be yourself, try your hardest, don't be scared, and act according to your conscience. In that, there's no need to regret anything, including the end.

ENDNOTES

Some of the internet links in the endnotes may have been broken, and some websites may have been taken down or revised. The views expressed in this book are those of the author and do not reflect the official policy or position of the Department of the Army, the Department of Defense, or the US government. The information in this book is from open sources.

1 Ian Stewart, *In Pursuit of the Unknown: 17 Equations That Changed the World* (New York: Basic Books, 2013).

2 Jim Collins, *Good to Great: Why Some Companies Make the Leap and Others Don't* (New York: HarperCollins, 2001), 91.

3 Ibid., 30.

4 Kate Isaacs and Allison Neale, "The Flywheel Philosophy," *strategy-business*, September 20, 2018, https://www.strategy-business.com/article/The-Flywheel-Philosophy.

5 Jim Collins, "The Flywheel Effect," Turning the Flywheel, jimcollins.com, https://www.jimcollins.com/concepts/the-flywheel.html.

6 David Lubinski and Camilla P. Benbow, "Intellectual Precocity: What Have We Learned Since Terman?" *Gifted Child Quarterly* 65, no. 1 (2020): 3–28, https://cdn.vanderbilt.edu/vu-my/wp-content/uploads/sites/826/2013/02/05123527/Article-GCQ-Lubinski-Benbow-2020.pdf.

7 C. M. Mueller and C. S. Dweck, "Praise for Intelligence Can Undermine Children's Motivation and Performance," *Journal of Personality and Social Psychology 75, no. 1 (1998): 33–52, https://doi.org/10.1037/0022-3514.75.1.33.*

8 Adam Grant, "No, You Don't Get an A for Effort," *New York Times*, December 26, 2024, https://www.nytimes.com/2024/12/26/opinion/school-grades-a-quantity-quality.html.

9 Miki Toyama, "Is Grit Persistence Adaptive? Goal Pursuit Behavior When Faced with a Difficult Goal," *Personality and Individual Differences* 223 (2024): Article 112610, https://doi.org/10.1016/j.paid.2024.112610.

10 Grant.

11 Lubinski and Benbow, 12.

12 Ibid.

13 Ibid.

14 Michael Rosenwald, "Myron E. Ullman III, Executive Who Remade Macy's and J.C. Penney, Dies at 77," *New York Times*, August 20, 2024, https://www.nytimes.com/2024/08/20/business/myron-e-ullman-iii-dead.html.

15 Ibid.

16 Ibid.

17 Ibid.

18 Chris Lange, "Every Helicopter in the US Military," 24/7 Wall St., June 16, 2023, https://247wallst.com/special-report/2023/06/16/every-helicopter-in-the-us-military.

19 Defense Advisory Committee on Women in the Services, "RFI 5a: Women in Aviation – Rated," December 4, 2019. The Department of Defense eliminated the Committee on November 18, 2025. See Federal Register, Department of Defense, https://www.federalregister.gov/documents/2025/11/18/2025-20198/termination-of-department-of-defense-federal-advisory-committee-defense-advisory-committee-on-women. The link to the original citation was deleted.

20 Tim Bakken, *The Cost of Loyalty: Dishonesty, Hubris, and Failure in the U.S. Military* (New York: Bloomsbury, 2020), 196, note 60.

21 E. Parada-Cabaleiro, M. Mayerl, S. Brandl, et al., "Song Lyrics Have Become Simpler and More Repetitive Over the Last Five Decades," *Scientific Reports* 14, 5531 (2024), 2, https://doi.org/10.1038/s41598-024-55742-x.

22 Ibid.

23 Rachel Kleinfeld, "Polarization, Democracy, and Political Violence in the United States: What the Research Says," Carnegie Endowment for International Peace, September 5, 2023, https://carnegieendowment.org/

research/2023/09/polarization-democracy-and-political-violence-in-the-united-states-what-the-research-says?lang=en.

24 Ibid.

25 Jennifer McCoy and Benjamin Press, "What Happens When Democracies Become Perniciously Polarized?" Carnegie Endowment for International Peace, January 18, 2022, https://carnegieendowment.org/research/2022/01/what-happens-when-democracies-become-perniciously-polarized?lang=en.

26 Jennifer McCoy, Benjamin Press, Murat Somer, and Ozlem Tuncel, "Reducing Pernicious Polarization: A Comparative Historical Analysis of Depolarization." Carnegie Endowment for International Peace, May 5, 2022, https://carnegieendowment.org/research/2022/05/reducing-pernicious-polarization-a-comparative-historical-analysis-of-depolarization?lang=en.

27 E. Parada-Cabaleiro, 2.

28 "No Fare: The Costs of MTA Fare and Toll Evasion," Citizens Budget Commission, September 11, 2025, https://cbcny.org/research/no-fare.

29 Taylor Robinson, "Fare Evasion Cost the M.T.A. $1 Billion in 2024, but the Trend May Be Slowing," *New York Times*, September 11, 2025, https://www.nytimes.com/2025/09/11/nyregion/fare-evasion-mta-subway-bus.html.

30 Rachel Weiner, "70% of Bus Riders in D.C. Area Don't Pay. Here's What Metro Is Doing About It," *Washington Post*, October 9, 2024, https://www.washingtonpost.com/dc-md-va/2024/10/08/metro-bus-dc-fare-evasion/.

31 Emma G. Fitzsimmons and Edgar Sandoval, "1 in 5 Bus Riders in New York City Evades the Fare, Far Worse than Elsewhere," *New York Times*, April 13, 2019, https://www.nytimes.com/2019/04/13/nyregion/mta-bus-riders-fare-beaters.html.

32 Nicole Napoli, "For Younger Women, Mental Health Now May Predict Heart Health Later," American College of Cardiology, March 28, 2024, https://www.acc.org/About-ACC/Press-Releases/2024/03/28/12/03/for-younger-women-mental-health-now-may-predict-heart-health-later.

33 Hamid Noghanibehambari and Jason Fletcher, "In Utero and Childhood Exposure to Alcohol and Old Age Mortality: Evidence from the Temperance Movement in the US," *Economics & Human Biology* 50 (2023): 101276, https://doi.org/10.1016/j.ehb.2023.101276.

[34] Jiaquan Xu, Sherry L. Murphy, Kenneth D. Kochanek, and Elizabeth Arias, "Mortality in the United States, 2024," National Center for Health Statistics, No. 585, January 26, 2026, https://www.cdc.gov/nchs/data/databriefs/db548.pdf.

[35] Shameek Rakshit and Matthew McGough, "How Does U.S. Life Expectancy Compare to Other Countries?" Peterson-KFF Health System Tracker, January 31, 2025, https://www.healthsystemtracker.org/chart-collection/u-s-life-expectancy-compare-countries/.

[36] The Global Economy, "Homicide rate – Country rankings" (1994-2017) (last accessed on February 1, 2026), https://www.theglobaleconomy.com/rankings/homicide_rate/.

[37] Amy Shira Teitel, "What Caused the Challenger Disaster?" History.com, January 25, 2018, https://www.history.com/articles/how-the-challenger-disaster-changed-nasa.

[38] Gary Stephenson, "How Weather Caused the Loss of the Space Shuttle Challenger," *Spectrum News*, January 29, 2021, https://spectrumlocalnews.com/weather/2021/01/19/how-weather-caused-the-loss-of-the-space-shuttle-challenger.

[39] Tom Minter, "Space Shuttle Challenger Explosion," CNN, January 28, 1986, https://www.google.com/search?q=Space+Shuttle+Challenger+Explosion%2C%E2%80%9D+YouTube%2C+CNN%2C+youtube.com&oq=Space+Shuttle+Challenger+Explosion%2C%E2%80%9D+YouTube%2C+CNN%2C+youtube.com&gs_lcrp=EgZjaHJvbWUyBggAEEUYOdIBDTI1NjY4OTk3OGowajCoAgCwAgA&sourceid=chrome&ie=UTF-8#fpstate=ive&vld=cid:ad208fba,vid:AfnvFnzs91s,st:0.

[40] James Glanz and John Schwartz, "Dogged Engineer's Effort to Assess Shuttle Damage," *New York Times*, September 26, 2003, https://www.nytimes.com/2003/09/26/us/dogged-engineer-s-effort-to-assess-shuttle-damage.html.

[41] *Ramasamy Venugopal,* "The Space Shuttle Columbia Disaster," *Space Safety Magazine* (last accessed February 1, 2026), https://www.spacesafetymagazine.com/space-disasters/columbia-disaster/.

[42] Dwayne A. Day, "Columbia Retold, and Untold," *The Space Review*, May 28, 2024, https://www.thespacereview.com/article/4800/1.

[43] "A Failure to 'Speak Up' in Meetings and the Catastrophic Columbia Space Shuttle Disaster," Hesper GRC, November 6, 2024, https://www.

hespergrc.com/news/a-failure-to-speak-up-in-meetings-and-the-catastrophic-columbia-space-shuttle-disaster/.

44 Ibid.

45 Kristin Fisher and Ashley Strickland, "Boeing Starliner's Crew Is Now on the Space Station After Encountering New Issues en Route," CNN, June 6, 2024, https://www.cnn.com/2024/06/06/science/boeing-starliner-new-helium-leaks-scn.

46 Morgan Smith, "The No. 1 Trait That Sets Highly Successful People Apart, Says Harvard Expert: 'It's Rare to Find,'" CNBC, June 23, 2024, https://www.cnbc.com/2024/06/23/the-no-1-trait-that-sets-highly-successful-people-apart-says-harvard-expert.html.

47 David Hambling, "Ukraine's Elegantly Simple Recoilless Shotgun Drone," *Forbes*, March 12, 2025, https://www.forbes.com/sites/davidhambling/2025/03/11/ukraines-elegantly-simple-recoilless-shotgun-drone/.

48 Alistair MacDonald and Ievgeniia Sivorka, "Hunting Russian Drones in a Prop Plane with Shotguns and Rifles," *Wall Street Journal*, August 24, 2025, https://www.wsj.com/world/ukraine-russia-drone-hunting-e2fea5fc.

49 David French, "'Ukraine Has Gone Through a Terrible Period': A Q. and A. with Frederick and Kimberly Kagan," *New York Times*, May 30, 2024, https://www.nytimes.com/2024/05/30/opinion/ukraine-russia-war-history.html.

50 Marcus Walker, Ian Lovett, and Ievgeniia Sivorka, "Ukraine's Once Nimble Army Is Mired in Soviet Decision-Making," *Wall Street Journal*, August 12, 2025, https://www.wsj.com/world/ukraine-russia-army-soviet-5fa8e1c9.

51 Ian Lovett and Nikita Nikolaienko, "It's Russian Men Against Ukrainian Machines on the Battlefields in Ukraine," *Wall Street Journal*, February 7, 2024, https://www.wsj.com/world/its-russian-men-against-ukrainian-machines-on-the-battlefields-in-ukraine-fcbe1592.

52 Benedict Vigers, "U.S.: Leader or Loser in the G7?," Gallup, April 17, 2024, https://news.gallup.com/poll/643598/leader-loser.aspx.

53 Ibid.

54 New York City Police Department, "CompStat," NYC.gov, January 19, 2026 through January 25, 2026 (last accessed February 1, 2026, https://www.nyc.gov/assets/nypd/downloads/pdf/crime_statistics/cs-en-us-city.pdf.

[55] "The Top 5 Most Corrupt U.S. Police Officers of All-Time," The Buzz Cincy, September 28, 2011, https://thebuzzcincy.com/1110132/the-top-5-most-corrupt-u-s-police-officers-of-all-time/.
[56] US Constitution, Article III, Section 3, Clause 1.
[57] Louis Eppolito and Bob Drury, *Mafia Cop: The Story of an Honest Cop Whose Family Was the Mob* (New York: Simon & Schuster, 1992).
[58] Benjamin Mueller, "New York City to Pay $5 Million in 'Mafia Cops' Case," *New York Times*, January 31, 2015, https://www.nytimes.com/2015/02/01/nyregion/new-york-city-to-pay-dollar5-million-in-mafia-cops-case.html.
[59] *United States v. Eppolito and Caracappa*, 543 F.3d 25, 29 (2nd Circuit, 2008).
[60] Daniel Schorn, "Mafia Cops?," *CBS News*, 60 Minutes, January 5, 2006, https://www.cbsnews.com/news/mafia-cops/.
[61] Mueller.
[62] Alan Feuer, "For 2 Ex-Detectives, Life Terms and Tales of Grief," *New York Times*, June 6, 2006, https://www.nytimes.com/2006/06/06/nyregion/for-2-exdetectives-life-terms-and-tales-of-grief.html.
[63] The Innocence Project, "Barry Gibbs" (last accessed April 13, 2026), https://innocenceproject.org/cases/barry-gibbs/.
[64] A. G. Sulzberger, "City to Pay $9.9 Million over Man's Imprisonment," *New York Times*, June 3, 2010, https://www.nytimes.com/2010/06/04/nyregion/04gibbs.html.
[65] Rocco Parascandola, "Mob Hit Eyed as Bronx Man Is Slain Walking Dog," *New York Post*, February 16, 2001, https://nypost.com/2001/02/16/mob-hit-eyed-as-bronx-man-is-slain-walking-dog/.
[66] See generally Mark Pendergrast, *Mirror Mirror: A History of the Human Love Affair with Reflection* (New York: Basic Books, 2004).
[67] "Taliban Bans 'Even the Sound of a Female Voice' in Public Across Afghanistan as UN Denounces New Virtue Laws," Australian Broadcasting Corporation, August 26, 2024, https://www.abc.net.au/news/2024-08-27/taliban-bans-womens-voices-faces-in-public-afghanistan-un/104273178.
[68] Donna Miles, "Bagram Hospital Provides Care to All Who Need It," *American Forces Press Service*, June 1, 2011, https://www.af.mil/News/Article-Display/Article/113192/bagram-hospital-provides-care-to-all-who-need-it/.
[69] Ibid.

70 Legal Information Institute, "hors de combat," Cornell Law School (last accessed February 1, 2026, https://www.law.cornell.edu/wex/hors_de_combat.

71 Maya Goldman, "More States Are Considering Allowing Medically Assisted Death This Year," *Axios*, February 9, 2024, https://www.axios.com/2024/02/09/medically-assisted-death-states.

72 "Does Morphine Make Death Come Sooner?" Canadian Virtual Hospice (last accessed February 1, 2026), https://www.virtualhospice.ca/en_US/Main+Site+Navigation/Home/Support/Support/Asked+and+Answered/Medications/Does+morphine+make+death+come+sooner_.aspx.

73 Dean Narciso and Bethany Bruner, "Franklin County Jury Finds Former Doctor William Husel Not Guilty on All 14 Murder Counts," *Columbus Dispatch*, April 20, 2022, https://www.dispatch.com/story/news/crime/2022/04/20/former-mount-carmel-doctor-william-husel-found-not-guilty/7269134001/.

74 Karl Albrecht, "The (Only) 5 Fears We All Share," *Psychology Today*, March 22, 2012, https://www.psychologytoday.com/us/blog/brainsnacks/201203/the-only-5-fears-we-all-share.

75 *Helvering v. Davis*, 301 U.S. 619, 641 (1937).

76 Aleksandra Dragutinovic, "US At-Will Employment States – Guide for 2025," Clockify, February 21, 2025, https://clockify.me/learn/business-management/at-will-employment-states/.

77 Dean Mobbs, Ralph Adolphs, Michael S. Fanselow, Lisa Feldman Barrett, Joseph E. LeDoux, Kerry Ressler, Kay M. Tye, and Nature Neuroscience, "On the Nature of Fear," *Scientific American*, October 10, 2019, https://www.scientificamerican.com/article/on-the-nature-of-fear/.

78 Leo Sands, "Scientists Say They've Discovered How the Brain Overcomes Fear," *Washington Post*, February 6, 2025, https://www.washingtonpost.com/science/2025/02/06/fear-human-brain-mouse-study/.

79 Elaine Eaker, Lisa Sullivan, Margaret Kelly-Hayes, Ralph D'Agostino, and Emilia Benjamin, "Marital Status, Marital Strain, and Risk of Coronary Heart Disease or Total Mortality: The Framingham Offspring Study," *Psychosomatic Medicine* 69, no. 6 (July–August 2007): 509–513, https://doi.org/10.1097/PSY.0b013e3180f62357.

80 Reporters Without Borders, "2024 World Press Freedom Index – Journalism Under Political pressure," https://rsf.org/en/index.

81 "Academic Freedom Index," Institute of Political Science at Friedrich-Alexander-Universität (last accessed February 1, 2026), https://academic-freedom-index.net.

82 "Academic Freedom Index, Update 2025," Institute of Political Science at Friedrich-Alexander-Universität, https://academic-freedom-index.net/research/Academic_Freedom_Index_Update_2025.pdf, 10-11.

83 James L. Gibson and Joseph L. Sutherland, "Keeping Your Mouth Shut: Spiraling Self-Censorship in the United States," *Political Science Quarterly 138, no. 3 (Fall 2023): 361–376*, https://doi.org/10.1093/psquar/qqad037.

84 Ibid.

85 "Investigation Report of the Airstrike on the Médecins Sans Frontières / Doctors Without Borders Trauma Center in Kunduz, Afghanistan on 3 October 2015," Just Security, https://www.justsecurity.org/wp-content/uploads/2022/02/Investigation-Report-of-the-Airstrike-on-the-Medecins-Sans-Frontieres-I-Doctors-Without-Borders-Trauma-Center-in-Kunduz-Afghanistan-on-3-October-2015-2016-report.pdf.

86 Simone Weichselbaum and Beth Schwartzapfel, "When Warriors Put on the Badge," The Marshall Project, March 30, 2017, https://www.themarshallproject.org/2017/03/30/when-warriors-put-on-the-badge.

87 Simone Weichselbaum, "Police with Military Experience More Likely to Shoot," The Marshall Project, October 15, 2018, https://www.themarshallproject.org/2018/10/15/police-with-military-experience-more-likely-to-shoot.

88 Department of Defense, "Annual Report on Suicide in the Military," 2023, https://www.dspo.mil/Portals/113/2024/documents/annual_report/ARSM_CY23_final_508c.pdf, 9.

89 National Center for Health Statistics, "Suicide and Self-harm," Centers for Disease Control, 2023, https://www.cdc.gov/nchs/fastats/suicide.htm.

90 Department of Defense, 9.

91 Ibid., 27.

92 Ibid., 14.

93 Jeffrey Allen Smith, Michael Doidge, Ryan Hanoa, and B. Christopher Frueh, "A Historical Comparison of U.S. Army & U.S. Civilian Suicide Rates, 1900–2020," *Psychiatry Research* 323 (May 2023): 115182, https://doi.org/10.1016/j.psychres.2023.115182.

94 Tim A. Bullman, Fatema Z. Akhtar, and Sybil W. Morley, et al., "Suicide Risk Among US Veterans with Military Service During the Vietnam War," *JAMA Network Open* 6, no. 12 (December 28, 2023): e2347616, https://doi.org/10.1001/jamanetworkopen.2023.47616.

95 Jeffrey T. Howard, Ian J. Steward, and Megan E. Amuan, et al., "Trends in Suicide Rates among Post-9/11 US Military Veterans with and without Traumatic Brain Injury from 2006–2020," *JAMA Neurology* 80, no. 9 (August 28, 2023): 889–896, https://doi.org/10.1001/jamaneurol.2023.2893.

96 Andrew R. Morral, Terry L. Schell, and Rosanna Smart, "Comparison of Suicide Rates among US Veteran and Nonveteran Populations," *JAMA Network Open* 6, no. 7 (July 18, 2023): e2324191, https://doi.org/10.1001/jamanetworkopen.2023.24191.

97 "Public Mass Shootings: Database Amasses Details of a Half Century of U.S. Mass Shootings with Firearms, Generating Psychosocial Histories," National Institute of Justice, February 3, 2022, https://nij.ojp.gov/topics/articles/public-mass-shootings-database-amasses-details-half-century-us-mass-shootings.

98 National Consortium for the Study of Terrorism and Responses to Terrorism, University of Maryland, "Profiles of Individual Radicalization in the United States (PIRUS) Mass Casualty Extremist Offenders with U.S. Military Backgrounds," June 2023, https://www.start.umd.edu/sites/default/files/publications/local_attachments/PIRUS-Mass%20Casualty%20Extremist%20Offenders%20with%20Military%20Background-Final%20%284%29.pdf, 2.

99 Jasper Cravens, "Inside Pete Hegseth's Civilian Purge at West Point," *Politico*, August 28, 2025, https://www.politico.com/news/magazine/2025/08/28/pete-hegseth-civilians-west-point-00523613.

100 Tim Bakken, *The Cost of Loyalty: Dishonesty, Hubris, and Failure in the U.S. Military* (New York: Bloomsbury, 2020), 187–188.

101 Luis Martinez, "Pentagon to Make Changes at Military Service Academies to Stem Sexual Assaults," *ABC News*, August 17, 2023, https://abcnews.go.com/Politics/pentagon-make-military-service-academies-stem-sexual-assaults/story?id=102346817.

102 See Bakken, 218, and Seymour M. Hersh, *Chain of Command: The Road from 9/11 to Abu Ghraib* (New York: HarperCollins, 2004), 2–3.

103 Jeremy Nobel, *Project UnLonely: Healing Our Crisis of Disconnection* (New York: Avery, 2023), 3.

104 Greg Jaffe, "The Pentagon's Culture Wars Strike West Point," *New York Times*, May 8, 2025, https://www.nytimes.com/2025/05/08/us/politics/west-point-hegseth-culture-wars.html.

105 Graham Parsons, "West Point Is Supposed to Educate, Not Indoctrinate," *New York Times*, May 8, 2025, https://www.nytimes.com/2025/05/08/opinion/west-point-trump-military.html.

106 Christina Shaw, "Pete Hegseth Says West Point Professor Who Resigned over Trump Admin Education Overhaul 'Will Not Be Missed,'" *New York Post*, May 9, 2025, https://nypost.com/2025/05/09/us-news/pete-hegseth-comments-on-west-point-usma-professor-graham-parson-retirement-decision/.

107 Timur Kuran, "Now Out of Never: The Element of Surprise in the East European Revolution of 1989," *World Politics* 44 (October 1991), 7–48, reprinted Cambridge University Press, October 1991, https://www.rochelleterman.com/ComparativeExam/sites/default/files/Bibliography%20and%20Summaries/Kuran%201991.pdf, 18-19.

108 Ibid., 30.

109 "Free to Think: Report of the Scholars at Risk Academic Monitoring Project," Scholars at Risk Network, 2025, https://www.scholarsatrisk.org/resources/free-to-think-2025/.

110 Ibid.

111 Richard Feynman, "'The First Principle Is That You Must Not Fool Yourself': Cargo-Cult Science Speech, Caltech, 1974," Speakola, https://speakola.com/grad/richard-feynman-caltech-1974.

112 Ryan Sweazey, "Whistle Blown, Three Years On," *The DoD Times (Redacted),* 60, Walk the Talk Foundation, March 1, 2025, https://walkthetalkfoundation.org/wp-content/uploads/60_DoDTR_Whistle-Blown-Three-Years-On.pdf.

113 Garry Kasparov, "How Russians and the West Failed Navalny," *Wall Street Journal*, February 19, 2024, https://www.wsj.com/opinion/how-russians-and-the-west-failed-navalny-putin-prison-regime-ukraine-biden-0bc32803.

114 Lewis Sorley, "To Change a War: General Harold K. Johnson and the PROVN Study," *Parameters* 28, no. 1 (Spring 1998): 93–109, https://doi.org/10.55540/0031-1723.1868.

115 Roger Ebert, "Apocalypse Now," RogerEbert.com, November 28, 1999, https://www.rogerebert.com/reviews/great-movie-apocalypse-now-1979.

116 "Al Haig and the Reagan Assassination Attempt—'I'm in Control Here,'" Association for Diplomatic Studies and Training (last accessed February 1, 2026), https://adst.org/2014/03/al-haig-and-the-reagan-assassination-attempt-im-in-charge-here/.

117 Wayne A. Hall, "Navy Officer Gets 7 Years for Sexual Assault at West Point," *Times Herald Record*, April 19, 2001, https://www.recordonline.com/story/news/2001/04/19/navy-officer-gets-7-years/51189051007/.

118 See Bruce Fleming, "Let's Abolish West Point: Military Academies Serve No One, Squander Millions of Tax Dollars," *Salon*, January 5, 2015, https://www.salon.com/2015/01/05/lets_abolish_west_point_military_academies_serve_no_one_squander_millions_of_tax_dollars/, and Tim Bakken, "Corruption in the U.S. Military Academies Is Harming Our National Security," *The American Conservative*, March 9, 2020, https://www.theamericanconservative.com/corruption-in-u-s-military-academies-is-harming-our-national-security/.

119 Institute for Education Sciences, "IPEDS Data Feedback Report 2024" (last accessed February 1, 2026), https://nces.ed.gov/IPEDS/DFR/2024/ReportHTML.aspx?unitid=226471, 13.

120 US Military Academy Annual Report, "United States Military Academy Board of Visitors Meeting 14 June 2012," https://www.westpoint.edu/bov/siteassets/meeting%20minutes/Signed%20Meeting%20Minutes%2020120614.pdf (link broken).

121 Tim Bakken, *The Cost of Loyalty: Dishonesty, Hubris, and Failure in the U.S. Military* (New York: Bloomsbury, 2020), 63.

122 Trisha Dach, "Is the West Point Acceptance Rate Accurate?" Gain Service Academy Admission, (last accessed February 1, 2026). https://www.gainserviceacademyadmission.com/west-point-acceptance-rate.

123 "United States Military Academy" (Test Scores and Acceptance) (last accessed February 1, 2026, https://collegescorecard.ed.gov/school/?197036-United-States-Military-Academy.

124 Michael S. Rosenwald, "J. Robin Warren, Who Proved That Bacteria Cause Ulcers, Dies at 87," *New York Times*, August 9, 2024, https://www.nytimes.com/2024/08/09/health/j-robin-warren-dead.html.

125 "The Nobel Prize in Physiology or Medicine 2024," The Nobel Prize, October 7, 2024, https://www.nobelprize.org/prizes/medicine/2024/press-release/.

126 Teddy Rosenbluth and Derrick Bryson Taylor, "Discovery in Tiny Worm Leads to Nobel Prize in Physiology or Medicine for 2 Scientists," *New*

York Times, October 7, 2024, https://www.nytimes.com/2024/10/07/health/nobel-prize-medicine.html.

127 US Census, "U.S. and World Population Clock," (last accessed February 1, 2026, https://www.census.gov/popclock/world.

128 Duygu Ağagündüz, et al., "Understanding the Role of the Gut Microbiome in Gastrointestinal Cancer: A Review," *Frontiers in Pharmacology* 14 (January 24, 2023): 1130562; correction regarding funding published July 30, 2025, https://doi.org/10.3389/fphar.2023.1130562.

129 See generally Saloni Dattani, Veronika Samborska, Hannah Roser, and Max Roser, "Cancer," Our World in Data (last accessed February 1, 2026), https://ourworldindata.org/cancer.

130 GBD 2021 Antimicrobial Resistance Collaborators (Christopher J. L. Murray et al.), "Global Burden of Bacterial Antimicrobial Resistance 1990–2021: A Systematic Analysis with Forecasts to 2050," *Lancet*, 404, no. 10459 (September 28, 2024): 1199–1226, https://www.thelancet.com/journals/lancet/article/PIIS0140-6736(24)01867-1/fulltext.

131 Lizette Ortega, "Antibiotic Resistance Could Cause Over 39 Million Deaths by 2050, Study Says," *Washington Post*, September 16, 2024, https://www.washingtonpost.com/science/2024/09/16/antibiotic-resistance-39-million-deaths-2050-study/.

132 David Lubinski and Camilla P. Benbow, "Intellectual Precocity: What Have We Learned Since Terman?" *Gifted Child Quarterly* 65, no. 1 (2020): 3–28, https://doi.org/10.1177/0016986220925447.

133 Ibid.

134 Carol Loomis, "The Inside Story of Warren Buffet," *Fortune*, April 11, 1988, https://fortune.com/article/warren-buffett-inside-story/.

135 Ibid.

136 Ibid.

137 Ibid.

138 Helen Ouyang, "The Race to Reinvent CPR," *New York Times Magazine*, March 27, 2024, https://www.nytimes.com/2024/03/27/magazine/ecpr-cardiac-arrest-cpr.html.

139 Ibid.

140 Ibid.

141 Ibid.

142 Ibid.

[143] R. Monica Klevens, Jonathan R. Edwards, Chesley L. Richards Jr., Teresa C. Horan, Robert P. Gaynes, Daniel A. Pollock, and Denise M. Cardo, "Estimating Health Care-Associated Infections and Deaths in U.S. Hospitals, 2002," *Public Health Reports* 122, no. 2 (March–April 2007): 160–166, https://doi.org/10.1177/003335490712200205.

[144] Ouyang.

[145] Arthur T. Coumbe, Steven J. Condly, and William L. Skimmyhorn, *Still Soldiers and Scholars? An Analysis of Army Officer Testing* (Carlisle, PA: US Army War College Press, December 15, 2017), https://press.armywarcollege.edu/cgi/viewcontent.cgi?article=1000&context=monographs, 12.

[146] Annika Weder, "Q&A – What Is Intelligence?" *Johns Hopkins Medicine*, October 5, 2020, https://www.hopkinsmedicine.org/news/articles/2020/10/qa--what-is-intelligence.

[147] Roberto Colom, Sherif Karama, Rex E. Jung, and Richard J. Haier, "Human Intelligence and Brain Networks," *Dialogues in Clinical Neuroscience* 12, no. 4 (2010): 489–501, https://doi.org/10.31887/DCNS.2010.12.4/rcolom.

[148] Joseph Pisani, "ACT Scores Fell for Class of 2023, Sixth Consecutive Decline," *Wall Street Journal*, October 11, 2023, https://www.wsj.com/us-news/education/act-test-scores-decline-for-class-of-2023-52dad941.

[149] Jane Nam, "All About SAT Scores: National Average and Full Statistics," Best Colleges (last accessed February 1, 2026, https://www.bestcolleges.com/research/average-sat-score-full-statistics/.

[150] Matt Barnum and Sara Randazzo, "American Kids Are Getting Even Worse at Reading," *Wall Street Journal*, January 29, 2025, https://www.wsj.com/us-news/education/reading-test-scores-american-students-5fb78d4e.

[151] "2019 NAEP High School Transcript Study (HSTS) Results," The Nation's Report Card, https://www.nationsreportcard.gov/hstsreport/#home.

[152] Giulia McDonnell Nieto del Rio, "University of California Will No Longer Consider SAT and ACT Scores," *New York Times*, May 15, 2021, https://www.nytimes.com/2021/05/15/us/SAT-scores-uc-university-of-california.html.

[153] Michael Hiltzik, "Is UCLA a 'Failed Medical School'? Debunking a Dumb Right-Wing Meme," *Los Angeles Times*, May 30, 2024, https://

www.latimes.com/business/story/2024-05-30/is-ucla-a-failed-medical-school-debunking-a-dumb-right-wing-meme.

[154] Aaron Sibarium, "'A Failed Medical School': How Racial Preferences, Supposedly Outlawed in California, Have Persisted at UCLA," *Washington Free Beacon*, May 23, 2024, https://freebeacon.com/campus/a-failed-medical-school-how-racial-preferences-supposedly-outlawed-in-california-have-persisted-at-ucla/.

[155] Ibid.

[156] UCLA David Geffen School of Medicine, "Phase 2 Grading Policy – Core Clerkships," 2023, https://medschool.ucla.edu/education/md-education/current-students/handbook-and-policies/assessment-and-grading/phase-2-grading-policy-core-clerkships.

[157] Lewis Pennock, "They're Going to Change the White Coat Next," *Daily Mail*, October 24, 2022, https://www.dailymail.co.uk/news/article-11348775/Top-doctor-slams-University-Minnesota-medical-school-abandoning-Hippocratic-oath.html.

[158] Zach Greenberg, "University of Minnesota Medical School Swears Off Compelled Speech in White Coat Ceremony," Foundation for Individual Rights and Expression, October 20, 2022, https://www.thefire.org/news/university-minnesota-medical-school-swears-compelled-speech-white-coat-ceremony.

[159] Brad N. Greenwood, Rachel R. Hardeman, Laura Huang, and Aaron Sojourner, "Physician–Patient Racial Concordance and Disparities in Birthing Mortality for Newborns," *Proceedings of National Academy of Science* 117, no. 35 (2020): 21194–21200, https://doi.org/10.1073/pnas.1913405117.

[160] Ibid.

[161] Ibid.

[162] Rob Picheta, "Black Newborns More Likely to Die When Looked After by White Doctors," CNN, August 20, 2020, https://www.cnn.com/2020/08/18/health/black-babies-mortality-rate-doctors-study-wellness-scli-intl.

[163] Tonya Russell, "Mortality Rate for Black Babies Is Cut Dramatically When Black Doctors Care for Them after Birth, Researchers Say," *Washington Post*, January 13, 2021, https://www.washingtonpost.com/health/black-baby-death-rate-cut-by-black-doctors/2021/01/08/e9f0f850-238a-11eb-952e-0c475972cfc0_story.html.

[164] *Students for Fair Admission v. Harvard College*, 600 U.S. 181 (2023) (Jackson dissent, footnote 99).

[165] George J. Borjas and Robert VerBruggen, "Physician–Patient Racial Concordance and Newborn Mortality," *Proceedings of National Academy of Science* 121, no. 39 (September 16, 2024): e2409264121, https://doi.org/10.1073/pnas.2409264121.

[166] Ibid.

[167] Ibid.

[168] Usha Lee McFarling, "Study Challenges Finding That Black Babies Are More Likely to Survive under the Care of Black Physicians," STAT, October 23, 2024, https://www.statnews.com/2024/10/23/study-finding-physician-race-affects-black-infant-mortality-challenged/.

[169] Theodore Joyce, "Do Black Doctors Save More Black Babies?" *Proceedings of National Academy of Science* 121, no. 39 (September 16, 2024), https://www.pnas.org/doi/10.1073/pnas.2415159121.

[170] Ibid.

[171] Paul Bloom, "Why Progressives Should Question Their Favorite Scientific Findings," *Chronicle of Higher Education*, October 25, 2024, https://www.chronicle.com/article/why-progressives-should-question-their-favorite-scientific-findings.

[172] See David Leonhardt, "The Misguided War on the SAT," *New York Times*, January 7, 2024, https://www.nytimes.com/2024/01/07/briefing/the-misguided-war-on-the-sat.html; Lily Knezevich and Wayne Camara, "The LSAT Is Still the Most Accurate Predictor of Law School Success," Law School Admissions Council (last accessed February 1, 2026), https://www.lsac.org/data-research/research/lsat-still-most-accurate-predictor-law-school-success; Robert F. Jones and Maria Thomae-Forgues, "Validity of the MCAT in Predicting Performance in the First Two Years of Medical School," *Journal of Medical Education* 59, no. 6 (June 1984): 455–464, https://doi.org/10.1097/00001888-198406000-00001; and Joshua T. Hanson, et al., "The Validity of MCAT Scores in Predicting Students' Performance and Progress in Medical School: Results from a Multisite Study," *Academic Medicine* 97, no. 9 (September 2022): 1374–1384, https://doi.org/10.1097/ACM.0000000000004754.

[173] Vianney Gómez, "As Courts Weigh Affirmative Action, Grades and Test Scores Seen as Top Factors in College Admissions," Pew Research Center,

April 26, 2022, https://www.pewresearch.org/short-reads/2022/04/26/u-s-public-continues-to-view-grades-test-scores-as-top-factors-in-college-admissions/.

174 Craig Welch, "Washed Away," AARP, May 28, 2024, https://www.aarp.org/home-living/washed-away/.

175 Ibid.

176 Matthew Shaer, "Why Is the Loneliness Epidemic So Hard to Cure?" *New York Times Magazine*, August 27, 2024, https://www.nytimes.com/2024/08/27/magazine/loneliness-epidemic-cure.html.

177 Patrick Sharkey, "Homebound: The Long-Term Rise in Time Spent at Home Among U.S. Adults," *Sociological Science* 11 (2024): 553–578, 553, https://doi.org/10.15195/v11.a20.

178 Ibid., 569.

179 Ibid., 570.

180 Ibid., 572.

181 "Nearly Two-Thirds of U.S. Households Are Family Households," US Census Bureau, November 12, 2024, https://www.census.gov/newsroom/press-releases/2024/families-and-living-arrangements.html.

182 Sharkey, 572.

183 Karl Albrecht, "The (Only) 5 Fears We All Share," *Psychology Today*, March 22, 2012, https://www.psychologytoday.com/us/blog/brainsnacks/201203/the-only-5-fears-we-all-share.

184 Cigna, "Loneliness and the Workplace: 2020 U.S. Report," January 2020, https://www.multivu.com/players/English/8670451-cigna-2020-loneliness-index/docs/CignaReport_1579728920153-379831100.pdf, 3.

185 Ibid., 4.

186 Ibid., at 5–8, 12–13, 15, and 17.

187 Martina Luchetti, et al., "A Meta-Analysis of Loneliness and Risk of Dementia Using Longitudinal Data from >600,000 Individuals," *Nature Mental Health* 2, no. 11 (2024): 1350–1361, https://doi.org/10.1038/s44220-024-00328-9.

188 Paul Fronstin and M. Christopher Roebuck, "Use of Health Care Services for Mental Health Disorders and Spending Trends," Employee Benefits Research Institute, September 8, 2022, 5, https://www.ebri.org/docs/default-source/pbriefs/ebri_ib_569_mentalhealth-8sept22.pdf?sfvrsn=12bb382f_7.

[189] Robert D. Putnam, *Bowling Alone: The Collapse and Revival of American Community* (New York: Simon & Schuster, 2001), 183.
[190] Ibid., 184.
[191] Ibid., 187.
[192] Ibid., 184.
[193] Ian Corbin and Joe Waters, "What the Surgeon General Missed About America's Loneliness Epidemic," *Newsweek*, May 16, 2023, https://www.newsweek.com/what-surgeon-general-missed-about-americas-loneliness-epidemic-opinion-1800045.
[194] US Surgeon General, *Our Epidemic of Loneliness and Isolation: The U.S. Surgeon General's Advisory on the Healing Effects of Social Connection and Community* (Washington, DC: US Department of Health and Human Services, 2023), https://www.hhs.gov/sites/default/files/surgeon-general-social-connection-advisory.pdf, 4.
[195] Ibid., 14.
[196] Ibid., 17.
[197] Robert D. Putnam and Richard V. Reeves, "Boy Crisis of 2025, Meet the 'Boy Problem' of the 1900s," *New York Times*, August 15, 2025, https://www.nytimes.com/2025/08/15/opinion/men-boys-crisis-progressive-era.html.
[198] John F. Helliwell, Richard Layard, Jeffrey D. Sachs, Jan-Emmanuel De Neve, Lara B. Aknin, and Shun Wang (eds.), *World Happiness Report 2025*, University of Oxford: Wellbeing Research Centre, https://files.worldhappiness.report/WHR25.pdf?_gl=1*177bebu*_gcl_au*Mjc5NTgyNjkuMTc2OTk4MTgzMw, 162–163.
[199] Ibid., 163.
[200] Ibid., 167.
[201] Ibid., 195.
[202] Ibid., 224.
[203] Jonathan Haidt, *The Anxious Generation: How the Great Rewiring of Childhood Is Causing an Epidemic of Mental Illness* (New York: Penguin, 2024), 4.
[204] Ibid., 7.
[205] Ibid., 14.
[206] *The President and the Dragon* (film), directed by Waleed Eltayeb and Ian D. Murphy, 2024.
[207] Jiaquan Xu, Sherry L. Murphy, Kenneth D. Kochanek, and Elizabeth Arias, "Mortality in the United States, 2024," National Center for

Health Statistics, No. 585, January 26, 2026, https://www.cdc.gov/nchs/data/databriefs/db548.pdf.

208 Johann Staerk, et al., "Sexual Selection Drives Sex Difference in Adult Expectancy across Mammals and Birds," *Science Advances* 11, no. 40 (October 1, 2025), https://doi.org/10.1126/sciadv.ady8433.

209 Galina A. Erikson, et. al, "Whole-Genome Sequencing of a Healthy Aging Cohort," *Cell* 165, no. 4 (2016): 1002–1011, https://doi.org/10.1016/j.cell.2016.03.022.

210 Ibid.

211 Mohana Ravindranath, "A Longevity Expert's 5 Tips for Aging Well," *New York Times*, May 6, 2025, https://www.nytimes.com/2025/05/06/well/live/eric-topol-longevity-tips.html.

212 Editors, "Enlightenment," *History.com*, https://www.history.com/articles/enlightenment.

213 Peter N. Stearns, "The History of Happiness," *Harvard Business Review*, January–February 2012, https://hbr.org/2012/01/the-history-of-happiness.

214 Ibid.

215 "Author Talks: The World's Longest Study of Adult Development Finds the Key to Happy Living," McKinsey & Company, February 16, 2023, https://www.mckinsey.com/featured-insights/mckinsey-on-books/author-talks-the-worlds-longest-study-of-adult-development-finds-the-key-to-happy-living.

216 Joshua Wolf Shenk, "What Makes Us Happy?" *The Atlantic*, June 1, 2009, https://www.theatlantic.com/magazine/archive/2009/06/what-makes-us-happy/307439/.

217 Ibid.

218 Greg Iacurci, "This Retirement Planning Gap Is 'Hidden in Plain Sight,' Harvard Professor Says," CNBC, May 29, 2024, https://www.cnbc.com/2024/05/29/this-retirement-planning-gap-is-hidden-in-plain-sight.html.

219 McKinsey.

220 John Robin, "The Grant Study," *Highbrow*, https://gohighbrow.com/the-grant-study/.

221 Ibid.

222 Daniel Kahneman, *Thinking, Fast and Slow* (New York: Farrar, Straus, 2011), 398.

223 Ibid., 399.

[224] Ibid., 400–401.

[225] Charlie Huntington, Scott M. Stanley, Brian D. Doss, and Galena K. Rhoades, "Happy, Healthy and Wedded? How the Transition to Marriage Affects Mental and Physical Health," *Journal of Family Psychology* 36, no. 4 (2021): 608–617, https://doi.org/10.1037/fam0000913.

[226] Ibid.

[227] Kahneman, 400.

[228] Helliwell, 81.

[229] Ibid., 82.

[230] Ibid., 62.

[231] Ibid., 98.

[232] Ibid., 139.

[233] Ibid., 146.

[234] Steve Russell, "Life Advice from Willie Nelson," *Men's Journal*, April 29, 2019, https://www.mensjournal.com/entertainment/life-advice-from-willie-nelson-w475661.

[235] Peter K. Jonason, Norman P. Li, and Laura Madson, "It is not all about the Benjamins: Understanding preferences for mates with resources," *Personality and Individual Differences* 52 (2012): 306-310, https://nebula.wsimg.com/6cdfa98355598593c647bd7e53c3fdd9?AccessKeyId=551B837F51991F7BBBCC&disposition=0&allow origin=1.

[236] David Ludden, "Do Women Really Prefer Men with Money over Looks?," *Psychology Today*, July 6, 2019, https://www.psychologytoday.com/us/blog/talking-apes/201907/do-women-really-prefer-men-with-money-over-looks.

[237] Yi Ming Li, Jian Li, Darius K. S. Chan, and Bo Zhang, "When Love Meets Money: Priming the Possession of Money Influences Mating Strategies," *Frontiers in Psychology* 7 (2016): 387, https://doi.org/10.3389/fpsyg.2016.00387.

[238] Ludden.

[239] Helliwell, 17–19.

[240] Daniel Kahneman and Angus Deaton, "High Income Improves Evaluation of Life but Not Emotional Well-Being," *Proceedings of the National Academy of Sciences* 107, no. 38 (2010): 16489–16493, https://doi.org/10.1073/pnas.1011492107.

[241] "Does More Money Correlate with Greater Happiness?" Penn Today, March 6, 2023, https://penntoday.upenn.edu/news/does-more-money-correlate-greater-happiness-Penn-Princeton-research.

[242] Matthew A. Killingsworth, Daniel Kahneman, and Barbara Mellers, "Income and Emotional Well-Being: A Conflict Resolved," *Proceedings of the National Academy of Sciences* https://www.pnas.org/doi/10.1073/pnas.2208661120.

[243] Penn Today.

[244] Ibid.

[245] Ibid.

[246] Killingsworth, Kahneman, and Mellers.

[247] Ibid.

[248] Richard Fry, "Are You in the American Middle Class? Find Out with Our Income Calculator," Pew Research Center, September 16, 2024, https://www.pewresearch.org/short-reads/2024/09/16/are-you-in-the-american-middle-class/.

[249] Joe Pinsker, "Money Buys Happiness, Even If You're Already Rich," *Wall Street Journal*, October 3, 2024, https://www.wsj.com/personal-finance/money-buys-happiness-even-if-youre-already-rich-51481105.

[250] Peter Gratton, "How Long Will It Take to Double Your Money? This Formula Shows You How," Investopedia, December 4, 2024, https://www.investopedia.com/financial-edge/0711/how-to-double-your-money-every-6-years.aspx.

[251] Patrick McGeehan, "New York City's Everlasting Scaffolding," *New York Times*, April 24, 2024, https://www.nytimes.com/2024/04/24/nyregion/nyc-scaffolding.html.

[252] Christopher Gray, "A Law and the Face of a City," *New York Times*, April 24, 2014, https://www.nytimes.com/2014/04/27/realestate/a-law-and-the-face-of-the-city.html.

[253] McGeehan.

[254] NOAA, "Can Humans Drink Seawater?" National Oceanic and Atmospheric Administration, https://oceanservice.noaa.gov/facts/drinksw.html.

[255] Model Penal Code, Section 3.02(1).

[256] Clare Ansberry and Anne Tergesen, "The Crushing Financial Burden of Aging at Home," *Wall Street Journal*, September 4, 2024, https://www.wsj.com/personal-finance/caregiving-aging-at-home-retirement-103520c7.

[257] Anne Kelly, et al, "Length of Stay for Older Adults Residing in Nursing Homes at the End of Life," *Journal of the American Geriatric Society* 58, no. 9 (2010): 1701–1706, https://doi.org/10.1111/j.1532-5415.2010.03005.x.

[258] Ibid.

[259] Robert J. Brent, "Life Expectancy in Nursing Homes," *Applied Economics* 54, no. 16 (2022): 1877–1888, https://doi.org/10.1080/00036846.2021.1983138.

[260] Ibid.

[261] Ibid.

[262] Ibid.

[263] Matthew A. Killingsworth, Daniel Kahneman, and Barbara Mellers, "Income and Emotional Well-Being: A Conflict Resolved," *Proceedings of the National Academy of Sciences* 120, no. 10 (2023): https://www.pnas.org/doi/10.1073/pnas.2208661120.

[264] Katie Engelhart, "Do Patients without a Terminal Illness Have the Right to Die?" *New York Times Magazine*, June 1, 2025, https://www.nytimes.com/2025/06/01/magazine/maid-medical-assistance-dying-canada.html.

[265] Barbie Latza Nadeau, "Switzerland Approves Assisted 'Suicide Capsule,'" The Daily Beast published via Yahoo News, December 6, 2021, https://www.yahoo.com/news/switzerland-approves-assisted-suicide-capsule-140255771.html.

[266] Katarzyna de Lazari-Radek and Peter Singer, "There's a Lesson to Learn from Daniel Kahneman's Death," *New York Times*, April 14, 2025, https://www.nytimes.com/2025/04/14/opinion/daniel-kahneman-death-suicide.html.

[267] Ibid.

[268] Oregon Health Authority, *2024 Oregon Death with Dignity Act, Data Summary*, (Oregon: Oregon Health Authority, March 27, 2025), https://www.oregon.gov/oha/PH/PROVIDERPARTNERRESOURCES/EVALUATIONRESEARCH/DEATHWITHDIGNITYACT/Documents/year27.pdf, 4.

[269] Ibid., 9.

[270] Lazari-Radek.

[271] Jason Zweig, "The Last Decision by the World's Leading Thinker on Decisions," *Wall Street Journal*, March 14, 2025, https://www.wsj.com/arts-culture/books/daniel-kahneman-assisted-suicide-9fb16124.

[272] Daniel Kahneman, *Thinking, Fast and Slow* (New York: Farrar, Straus, 2011), 386.

[273] Ibid., 388.

[274] Ibid.

[275] Zweig.

[276] Alex Koller, "Top 5 Regrets People Have on Their Deathbeds: What They Can Teach Us about Living Healthy, Fulfilled Lives, from an Internal Medicine Doctor," CNBC, September 23, 2024, https://www.cnbc.com/2024/09/23/regrets-people-have-at-end-of-lives-says-doctor-what-we-can-learn.html.

[277] Ashton Jackson, "People's Last Words Are Often These 4 Phrases: What They Teach Us about Living Happy, Meaningful Lives, from an Oncologist," CNBC, May 31, 2024, https://www.cnbc.com/2024/05/31/phrases-that-are-often-peoples-last-words-says-doctor-what-we-can-learn.html.

[278] Matthew Solan, "Learning to Right a Wrong," *Harvard Health Publishing*, May 1, 2022, https://www.health.harvard.edu/mind-and-mood/learning-to-right-a-wrong.

[279] "Author Talks: The World's Longest Study of Adult Development Finds the Key to Happy Living," McKinsey & Company, February 16, 2023, https://www.mckinsey.com/featured-insights/mckinsey-on-books/author-talks-the-worlds-longest-study-of-adult-development-finds-the-key-to-happy-living.

[280] Gary Saul Morson, "Leo Tolstoy's Search for the Meaning of Life," *Wall Street Journal*, August 14, 2025, https://www.wsj.com/opinion/leo-tolstoys-search-for-the-meaning-of-life-technology-death-17c08880.

[281] Ibid.

ACKNOWLEDGMENTS

I want to express my deep appreciation to Debby Englander, this book's editor, for believing in the book and that there is a way to help all of us become better decision-makers.

I'm extremely grateful to Lauren Campbell, the managing editor, for her guidance and for bringing the book to readers.

To literary agent Jeff Ourvan, of the Jennifer Lyons Literary Agency, thank you for your support and insight.

To everyone at Post Hill Press, thank you.

ABOUT THE AUTHOR

Tim Bakken is the first person promoted to, and the longest serving, Professor of Law at the US Military Academy, West Point (1802). He created the Department of Law at the National Military Academy of Afghanistan. A legally recognized whistleblower, he is one of the few federal employees to win a retaliation case against the US Army.

A former homicide prosecutor in New York City (Brooklyn), he has been a Fulbright Specialist and visiting professor or scholar at the University of Cambridge, University of Chile, University of Sydney, Australian National University, and Ural State Law University, Russia. He is a graduate of the law schools at the University of Wisconsin and Columbia University.